LESSONS
ON
LIBERTY

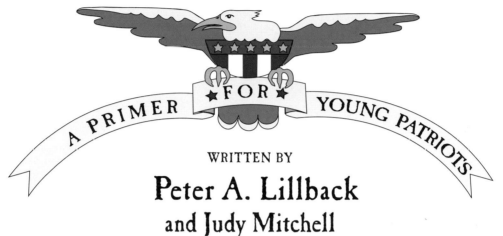

A PRIMER ✦ FOR ✦ YOUNG PATRIOTS

WRITTEN BY

Peter A. Lillback
and Judy Mitchell

❧ ADORN'D WITH DRAWINGS BY JUDY MITCHELL ❧

To Sophia Hernz,
I hope you enjoy
reading this book
as much as I enjoyed
writing & drawing it!
Judy Mitchell

An Early & Pleasant Guide to Our Country's History

Published by The Providence Forum, West Conshohocken, PA 19428

To Elie, Nancy and Bill with sincere gratitude.
PAL •~•

To my sweetheart... whose love and encouragement allows me to create.
•~• JM

Lessons on Liberty began with an engaging poem by author Peter Lillback and his avid interest and study of our nation's earliest flags. He reasoned, what better way to continue to instruct young minds in our country's rich heritage than to punctuate these two with a definition of a key word from his poem and corresponding quotes from the Bible and Poor Richard's Almanac?

To knit these diverse elements together, co-author and illustrator Judy Mitchell researched and created the facing pages. Believing the premise that history can be fascinating and fun, she followed paths that piqued her own curiosity and is sure it will excite the imaginations of readers young and old.

We would be remiss if we did not also acknowledge the help and support from staff. Our special thanks goes to Alexandra Thompson, Ralf Augstroze, Priscilla Lillback, Rebecca Courrier, Kate Kotanchek, Carolyn Jewett and Carolyn Giosa for their tireless efforts.

•~• **We hope you enjoy our labor of love!** •~•

THESE LESSONS ARE GRATEFULLY
DEDICATED TO
THREE SPECIAL FRIENDS
WITHOUT WHOSE
WISDOM, LOVE, GENEROSITY
AND ENTHUSIASM,
THIS PROJECT WOULD NEVER
HAVE BECOME A REALITY.

•~• THANK YOU •~•
ELIE, NANCY, AND BILL!

Table of Contents

Lessons on Liberty • A Primer for Young Patriots ᕬ
Copyright © 2007 by Peter A. Lillback and Judy Mitchell

ISBN: 0-9786052-8-4
ISBN13: 978-0-9786052-8-5

Unless otherwise indicated, all scripture references are from the King James version of the Bible (KJV).

All illustrations included are used by permission. Detailed credit list is included in the endnotes.

For Library of Congress Control Number, please contact the publisher.

Printed in the United States of America
2008 – First Edition

Providence Forum Press
The Providence Forum
One Tower Bridge
100 Front Street, Suite 1415
West Conshohocken, Pennsylvania 19428
(866) 55-FORUM
www.providenceforum.org

Before you begin...

Designed for all ages, *Lessons on Liberty* uses a simple alphabet poem to summarize the fundamental principles of American liberty.

On each letter page is a symbol of the history which that letter represents, along with an historically appropriate flag. As an early form of mass communication, flags served as public symbols of national aspirations as well as military signals. Some of the flag designs that are depicted in this book were lost to history and are here rediscovered for the first time.

Additional components on each letter page include three short elements for instruction. The first is a definition drawn from Noah Webster's 1828 *American Dictionary of the English Language*, produced during the years when the American home, church and school cooperated on a biblical and patriotic basis.

Enhancing these definitions are two of the greatest essential early American educational tools: the *Bible* and *Poor Richard's Almanack*. The *Bible*, more specifically the *Book of Proverbs*, was considered an essential text-book by all faiths in early America. It was the most widely accepted educational tool used to impart truth and wisdom. Verses from the *Bible* are marked by various symbols from the Judeo-Christian tradition, more fully defined in the back of the book. *Poor Richard's Almanack* was written by patriot and statesman Benjamin Franklin. It was an annually published collection of quotes, proverbs, sayings and observations from Franklin's voluminous reading and experiences. His words are marked by this symbol, taken from a woodcut which illustrated *The New England Primer,* the first widely-used American textbook for children, which also included an alphabet poem.

On the opposite page the reader will learn, through powerful quotes and surprising facts, truths about our nation's founding designed in an appealing, entertaining way for all ages.

Finally, the book includes activity pages to further teach young scholars with a "hands-on" approach to learning. Perforated for easy tear out, these pages can be reproduced on a copier.

James Madison once declared, *"The diffusion of knowledge is the only guardian of true liberty."* Please join with us at **The Providence Forum** in striving to preserve our unparalleled heritage of freedom for future generations by introducing them to the timeless truths found in *Lessons on Liberty: A Primer for Young Patriots.*

LESSONS ON LIBERTY
A PRIMER FOR YOUNG PATRIOTS

Lost and forgotten is our History,
Gone are the Lessons of our Liberty.
So listen to lessons that Patriots taught,
And you will remember what Liberty costs.

A is for AMERICA, a new world that's free.

B is for BRAVE PILGRIMS who sought liberty.

C is for CONSTITUTION, of our laws, the most high.

D is for DECLARATION on the Fourth of July.

E is for EAGLE that soars in the clouds.

F is for our FLAG that makes us so proud.

G is for GOD to our motto be true.

H is for HAPPINESS that we can pursue.

I is for INDEPENDENCE, self-government's new.

J is for JUSTICE so each gets his due.

K is for KINGS without royalty.

L is for the bell that's called LIBERTY.

M is for MILITARY that keeps us from harm.

N is for NATURE, our forests and farms.

O is for OPINIONS that we're free to say.

P is for PATRIOTS, who pointed the way.

Q is for QUEENS who've lost their command.

R is for REPUBLIC, representatives rule in our land.

S is for STARS on a field of blue.

T is for the TREE OF LIBERTY; from Boston it grew.

U is for U.S.A.; UNITED we'll stand.

V is for VIGILANCE which freedom demands.

W is for WASHINGTON, who's first in our hearts.

X is for EXPLORERS who discovered these parts.

Y is for YEARNING HEARTS crossing the sea.

Z is for ZEALOUS HEROES who love liberty.

LESSONS ON LIBERTY are needed by all,
Whether you're big or whether you're small.
So learn these true lessons and do learn them well,
Then all generations in freedom will dwell.

Lost and forgotten is our History,

Gone are the Lessons* of our Liberty.

So listen to lessons that Patriots taught,

And you will remember what Liberty costs.

The Fifty-Star Flag of the United States of America

*L ESSONS · Instruction or truth taught by experience; anything read or recited to a teacher by a pupil or learner for improvement.

❮⚬✳⚭✳⚭✳⚬❯

✗ *"Pay attention and listen to the sayings of the wise; apply your heart to what I teach."*

Proverbs 22:17

GENIUS WITHOUT EDUCATION IS LIKE SILVER IN THE MINE.

POOR RICHARD'S ALMANACK

Benjamin Franklin

"Let thy child's first lesson be obedience, and the second may be what thou wilt."

Benjamin Franklin (American statesman, scientist, philosopher, printer, writer, and inventor, 1706-1790)

The education of children was important even in the early days of the colonies. By law in the Massachusetts Bay Colony, one elementary school was mandated for towns with 50 families, one grammar school for towns of 100 families. New England Dame Schools were the first private elementary schools. Taught by women in their homes, they had no desks, maps or blackboards. It was the only school girls could attend.

When William Penn arrived in 1682, he found 6,000 Swedes had already set up a school in what is now Upland, PA. His *Law of 1683* required that anyone having charge of a child to make sure he or she could read and write by the age of 12 or face a £5 fine. In 1689, the Friends Public School was founded by Quakers for both sexes and all classes of people.Tuition to the school was free if a student couldn't afford it.

In the South the first school was started in 1636, when Benjamin Symms died and left 200 acres plus 8 cows for a free school in Elizabeth County. On southern plantations, a male tutor taught boys higher math, Greek, Latin, science, navigation, geography, history, fencing, social etiquette and plantation management. On the other hand, girls were taught by a governess, usually from England. They learned reading (so they could read the Bible), writing, arithmetic (to enter household expenses), art, music, French, social etiquette, needlework, weaving, and spinning.

From 1690 to the 19th century, *The New England Primer* was used extensively in early colonial America. Primarily religious, this small book (3 inches by 4 inches) was required reading for both church and school.

PRIMER BOSTON: 1777.

About 2 3/4 x 5 inches in size, **horn books** were paddle shaped boards with an attached paper sheet on which was written the alphabet (in upper and lower case letters), the Lord's Prayer, benediction, or a Scripture verse. It was then covered with a sheet of **pellucid** horn.

The word *"pellucid"* means transparent. Sheep or oxen horns were used. After being left in cold water for several weeks, the usable part would separate from the bone. It was then heated....first in boiling water, then by fire. The piece, pressed by plates, was made smooth and transparent.

A leather thong was attached to the bottom and was carried around the student's neck or hung from a belt.

NEW ENGLAND DAME SCHOOL
If you didn't know your lessons you were called a dunce, forced to wear a dunce cap, and sit on a dunce stool.

DUNCE

No people can be bound to acknowledge and adore the Invisible Hand which conducts the affairs of men more than the people of the United States. ....We ought to be no less persuaded that the propitious smiles of Heaven can never be expected on a nation that disregards *the eternal rules of order and right which Heaven itself has ordained.*

George Washington's Inaugural Address

The "external rules" Washington mentioned in his address were codified in the TEN COMMANDMENTS. Once included in the *New England Primer*, these "rules of order and right" listed below are from the 1843 edition. Written as a poem, they were easier to remember.

1. THOU shalt have no more gods but me.
2. Before no idol bend thy knee.
3. Take not the name of God in vain.
4. Dare not the Sabbath day profane,
5. Give both thy parents honor due.
6. Take heed that thou no murder do.
7. Abstain from words and deeds unclean.
8. Steal not, though thou be poor and mean.
9. Make not a wilful lie, nor love it.
10. What is thy neighbor's dare not covet.

DON'T MISS the bronze plaque of the 10 Commandments in the floor of the National Archives!

St. Andrew's Cross

...a Greek cross that's been rotated 45º, the St. Andrew's Cross is also known as *crux decussata.* (That's Latin for cross with honor, glory or distinction.) According to legend, Andrew, one of the twelve apostles, told his executioner he was not worthy to be crucified on the same type of cross as did his Lord, Jesus.

Our Judeo-Christian heritage is still evident in our nation's capitol.

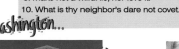
The 10 Commandments go to Washington...

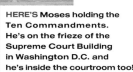

HERE'S Moses holding the Ten Commandments. He's on the frieze of the Supreme Court Building in Washington D.C. and he's inside the courtroom too!

SEE Moses with tablets overlooking the Reading Room at the Library of Congress...

With the admission of Hawaii as the 50th State of the Union, President Dwight Eisenhower issued an Executive Order on August 21,1959, which provided for the arrangement of stars in 9 rows staggered horizontally and 11 rows staggered vertically. This 27th flag of the United States became the official flag of our nation on July 4, 1960. Nine presidents have served under this flag.

 **is for America,* a new world that's free.**

Columbus sailed under this flag • Spain • 1492

* **A**MERICA • Derived from the name of Amerigo Vespucci, a native of Florence, Italy, who first recognized that what Columbus had discovered was a new continent and not just a part of Asia. ━━●∗◉∗●━

✟ *"Righteousness exalts a nation, but sin is a disgrace to any people."*
Proverbs 14:34

HAPPY THAT NATION, - FORTUNATE THAT AGE, WHOSE HISTORY IS NOT DIVERTING.
POOR RICHARD'S ALMANACK

The *Cross Patée* dates back from the Crusades and was used as a sign of divine protection.

✠

Columbus' flagship went aground on a coral reef and was destroyed in December 1492.

Niña
caravel

Pinta
caravel

Niña means "little girl" in Spanish; *Pinta* means "spot or mark." Of the 3 ships, Columbus preferred the *Niña* because she was faster and easier to maneuver. He logged more than 25,000 miles on her.

This is the banner under which Columbus sailed. The letter "F" stands for Ferdinand of Aragon and the "Y"(old Castilian didn't use "I" to begin words) stands for Isabella of Castile. Both kingdoms were united under the cross of Christianity. The lions and castles found on the flag of Spain are from the coat of arms of the kingdoms of Castile and Leon. Together, they symbolically represent the uniting of these two kingdoms.

A month after Columbus returned from his first voyage he began signing his name this way. A combination of Byzantine-Greek and Latin, it reads *Xpo ferens* ("Bearing Christ"). The top three lines of code in his signature have yet to be successfully deciphered.

Santa Maria
The *Santa Maria* was a *naõ* and was larger than the other two ships. It was named for the Virgin Mary.

WHAT DID THE WELL-DRESSED SAILOR PACK IN HIS TRUNK FOR THE FIRST TRANS-ATLANTIC CRUISE?

Seamen wore a red cap on land to distinguish themselves from farmers or laborers.

- three pairs of footwear
- four handkerchiefs
- one pair of underwear
- two shirts
- cloth tunic
- two overcoats

Chow time!

A champion thoroughbred race horse, **Sea Biscuit** became an American legend during the Depression.

Sea Biscuit?

Hardtack, or sea biscuit, was a hard-baked biscuit made of flour and water. Because they did not easily spoil, they were a staple food on the sea.

...yum yum

Café Santa Maria
(from Columbus' list of provisions)
- hardtack · salted meat
- fish (fresh & salted)
- olive oil · cheese · lentils
- beans · honey · rice
- almonds · raisins

Christopher Columbus and Amerigo Vespucci were both from Italy, and they knew each other. Vespucci personally assisted with the preparations of Columbus' second expedition in 1493. As Chief Navigator in Spain, he prepared official maps of newly-discovered lands and was the first to coin the phrase *Mundus Novus* or "New World." He recognized that what Columbus had discovered was a new continent, *not* just part of India or Asia as the explorer had thought.

In 1507, cartographer Martin Waldseemüeller published this map which designated this "fourth part of the world" as *America.* Vespucci is pictured on top of the map.

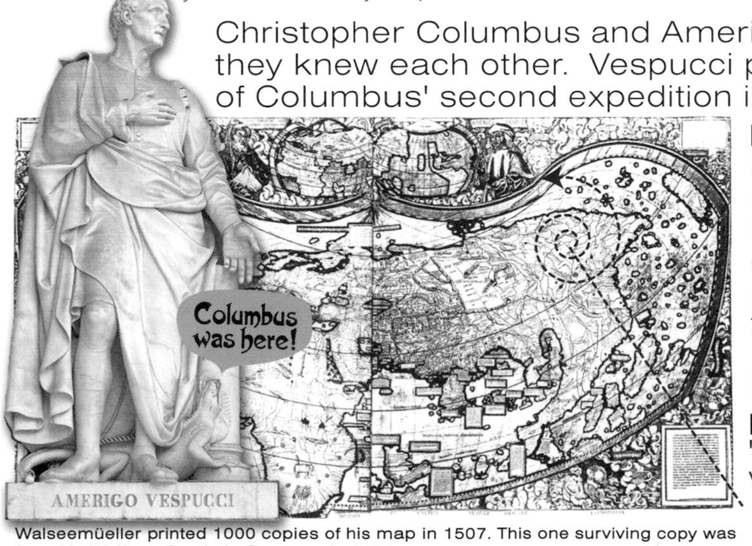

Columbus was here!

AMERIGO VESPUCCI

Walseemüeller printed 1000 copies of his map in 1507. This one surviving copy was found in Wolfegg Castle in Germany in 1901.

B is for Brave Pilgrims* who sought liberty.

Grand Union Flag: • the flag under which the Pilgrims sailed (1620)

* **PILGRIM** • A wanderer, a traveler; particularly one who travels a distance from his own country to visit a holy place.

"When the storm has swept by, the wicked are gone, but the righteous stand firm forever."
Proverbs 10:25

PROSPERITY DISCOVERS VICE; ADVERSITY, VIRTUE.

POOR RICHARD'S ALMANACK

The Pilgrims were originally called "Separatists" because they separated from the established church of England. Leaving England, the group settled in Holland, where they remained for 11 years. Fearful that their children would lose their English identity and still in search of religious freedom, the Separatists then left Holland on a small ship named the *Speedwell* and sailed back to England. There they joined other Separatists traveling on the *Mayflower*. When the *Speedwell* began to leak, all of the passengers crowded onto the *Mayflower.*

In September 1620, with a crew of 30 and 102 passengers, the *Mayflower* left Plymouth, England. The trip took 66 days, encountered many storms and saw 2 deaths and 1 birth. They were headed to Virginia (which at that time reached to present-day New York), but bad weather forced the ship to land on what is now called Cape Cod, Massachusetts.

The name *Mayflower* was a common name for ships sailing at that time. The trailing arbutus, or mayflower, is now the state flower of Massachusetts.

Epigaea repens

The cod has played an important role in Massachusetts. A carved model of the fish has hung in the State House in Boston since 1747. It points to the majority party.

The Pilgrims were helped by Squanto. Squanto's real name was *Tisquantum*, a native of the Pawtuxet tribe. He taught the Pilgrims how to plant and fish in their new land and helped them get along with the other Native Americans. While acting as guide and interpreter on William Bradford's expedition around Cape Cod, he contracted smallpox and died.

Flag of St. George
Flag of St. Andrew
Flag of St. Patrick

The Mayflower flew under the Grand Union, which combined the flags of England, Scotland, and Ireland, countries then ruled by James I.

It's all Algonquian to me!
Squanto's native tongue was Algonquian. Did you know that hickory, hominy, mocassin, moose, opossum, persimmon, raccoon, totem, wigwam, and woodchuck are all Algonquian words?

For the Pawtuxet, corn, or maize, was considered the most valued gift from their creator, Kiehtan.

In Algonquian, "oppossum" was *apasum* or *white animal.*

William Bradford, first governor
William Bradford

Contrary to popular myth, Pilgrims had no buckles on their hats, belts or shoes. They wore black only on Sundays or for formal occasions.

Pilgrim boys and girls wore wool or linen *gowns* or dresses like this, dyed yellow, red, blue, brown or green until they were 8 years old.

While the Pilgrims are famous for giving us Thanksgiving, that feast was only celebrated once by the Pilgrims in 1621. It did not become a national holiday until Abraham Lincoln made it so in 1863.

NAME THAT TURKEY!
a. Tom
b. Gobbler
c. Cock-turkey
d. Caruncle

The first three are correct. Caruncles are the funny looking things under the male turkey's neck.

The first feast included wild turkey, peas, corn, wheat, 5 deer, fish (bass and cod), and barley.

Pilgrims called cats "mousers." Instead of saying good-bye, they said, "God bye with you."

Phew..no moose on the menu!

C is for Constitution* of our laws, the most high.

* **CONSTITUTION** • A system of fundamental principles for the government of rational and social beings. In free states, the constitution is higher in authority than the statutes or laws enacted by the legislature and so it limits and controls its power.

"The law of the wise is a fountain of life."
Proverbs 13:14

WHERE THERE'S NO LAW, THERE'S NO BREAD.
POOR RICHARD'S ALMANACK

The American Constitution

The oldest and shortest written constitution of any government in the world, it is "the greatest single effort of national deliberation that the world has ever seen."

John Adams (1787)

Delaware was the first state to ratify the *Constitution,* followed by Pennsylvania and New Jersey. Rhode Island was the last of the original colonies to sign on... it was 3 years later!

From first to last...

1. Delaware (12/7/1787)
2. Pennsylvania (12/12/1787)
3. New Jersey (12/18/1787)
4. Georgia (1/2/1788)
5. Connecticut (1/9/1788)
6. Massachusetts (2/6/1788)
7. Maryland (4/28/1788)
8. South Carolina (5/23/1788)
9. New Hampshire (6/21/1788)
10. Virginia (6/25/1788)
11. New York (7/26/1788)
12. North Carolina (11/21/1789)
13. Rhode Island (5/29/1790)

This flag of 13 stars and 13 stripes flew at the Constitutional Convention in 1787. It was decided there that an additional star would be added for every state that joined the union thereafter.

James Madison, our fourth President, is considered *"the Father of the Constitution."* In 1779, at the age of 28, he was elected to the Continental Congress. For the next five years, he drew up treaties and implemented laws for his new country. He developed the Virginia Plan, which became the foundation of our *Constitution*. Later, with John Jay and Alexander Hamilton, he wrote *The Federalist,* a collection of 85 papers defining and defending the *Constitution*.

Oops! Pensylvania?

No, it's **NOT** a typographical error in the *Constitution*. The misspelling of the word **"Pensylvania"** above the signers' names is noticeable today; however, it seems that using one "n" for Pennsylvania was commonplace in colonial times...It was spelled **"Pensylvania"** on the Liberty Bell as well.

Of the 85 Federalist papers, Alexander Hamilton wrote 51, Madison wrote 26, and John Jay, 5. Madison and Hamilton jointly authored 2. The two most famous articles, Nos. 10 & 51, were written by Madison alone.

Franklin annually compiled a collection of sayings, quotes and observations and called it Poor Richard's Almanack.

As President, James Madison tried to declare Thanksgiving TWICE in 1815. Neither time was in the fall.

"I consent to this Constitution because I expect no better, and because I am not sure that it is not the best."

At 81, Benjamin Franklin was the oldest member of the Constitutional Convention. Because of his poor health, he needed help to sign the document. As he did so, tears streamed down his face.

While in office, President Madison appointed chaplains for the armed services.

Another version of the Cross Patée, this cross is commonly mistaken for the Maltese Cross, which looks like this.

How old was the youngest signer of the Constitution?

a. 43
b. 19
c. 26
d. 33

The answer is "c." There were 55 men at the Constitutional Convention; the average age was 43. Twenty-six-year-old Jonathan Dayton of New Jersey was the youngest signer.

is for Declaration* on the Fourth of July.

Betsy Ross Flag • the first "Stars & Stripes" created in 1777

*DECLARATION • A public announcement; proclamation; expression of facts, opinions, promises, predictions in writings. ━━━◦•✦◦✦•◦━━━

✝ *"Does not wisdom call out? Does not understanding raise her voice?"*

Proverbs 8:1

 MAN'S TONGUE IS SOFT, & BONE DOTH LACK; YET A STROKE THEREWITH MAY BREAK A MAN'S BACK.

POOR RICHARD'S ALMANACK

Fireworks, or **pyrotechnics**, were developed and used in warfare by the ancient Chinese. Introduced to Europe by the Arabs and Greeks, by the 17th century they had become a common part of celebrations. Through the use of chemicals, colors were added to the displays in the mid-18th century.

The fountain effect in fireworks is caused by the use of steel filings.

According to legend, John Hancock signed his name largely and clearly to be sure King George III could read it, causing his name to become an **eponym** for "signature." However, other examples show that Hancock always wrote his signature this way.

WHAT'S AN EPONYM? A person whose name is used metaphorically to signify a quality or thing. For example, the word *Sandwich* came from the Earl of Sandwich, who, not wishing to be called away from a game of cards, asked a servant to bring him a serving of meat between two slices of bread.

In 1776, there were no rules regulating the position of the stars on our flag. In 1818, Congress specified 13 stripes but set no pattern for the stars. It wasn't until 1912 that the "row" arrangement became official.

Did you know?...

That the *Declaration of Independence* has been a source of inspiration outside the United States? It encouraged Antonio de Nariño and Francisco de Miranda to strive to overthrow the Spanish empire in South America. The Marquis de Mirabeau quoted it enthusiastically during the French Revolution.

The *Declaration* was celebrated in Philadelphia on July 9th by a public reading and the ringing of church bells and the State House Bell (now called the Liberty Bell). It was not signed by all the delegates until a month later.

5 or 6 pointed stars?

Tradition says that when George Washington originally approached Betsy Ross about creating our first flag, he had with him a design which had 6-pointed stars. (After all, he had them on his own personal flags.) When the seamstress showed him with one snip of her scissors she could cut a 5-pointed one, he changed his mind and she got the job. *You too can cut a 5-pointed star with one snip in the activity pages.*

IN CONGRESS. JULY 4. 1776.

The "unanimous" line was added then by Timothy Matlack of Philadelphia.

Lap desk used by Jefferson to write the *Declaration.*

Who was the last person to sign the Declaration?

Thomas McKean of Delaware...he signed it in 1777.

This cross ✝ is primarily used in the Russian Orthodox Church. The slanted bar is said to come from the St. Andrew Cross. St. Andrew is believed to have brought Christianity to Russia.

For many years the *Declaration of Independence* had no permanent home. Twice, it narrowly missed being destroyed by fire and was almost captured during the Revolutionary War and the War of 1812. In 1894, it was put in a safe in the Department of State. In 1921, it was moved to the Library of Congress, where it remained until 1952. The document now resides in the National Archives in Washington, D.C.

Thomas Jefferson was a scholar and avid reader. His 10,000-volume library formed the foundation of the Library of Congress.

The *Declaration of Independence* was largely written by Thomas Jefferson. At the request of committee members John Adams, Benjamin Franklin, Roger Sherman, and Robert Livingstone, he wrote the first draft. Corrections and additions were made by Franklin and Adams.

is for Eagle * that soars in the clouds.

The original Eagle and Stripes, The Schuyler Flag • circa 1780

EAGLE • One of the largest species of fowl, has keen sight and preys on small animals, fish, etc... Due to the elevation of his aerial course, and the strength and rapidity of his wings in flight, he is called the king of birds. Hence the figure of an eagle was made the standard of the Romans, and the spread eagle is a principal figure in the arms of the U.S.

✝ *"Those who hope in the Lord will renew their strength. They will soar on wings like eagles; they will run and not grow weary, they will walk and not be faint."*

Isaiah 40:31

HE IS ILL CLOTHED THAT IS BARE OF VIRTUE.

POOR RICHARD'S ALMANACK

15

So who was General Schuyler?...

Philip John Schuyler originally served as a colonial officer for the British Army from 1755-58. He was a representative to the New York Assembly for eight years and was a delegate to the 2nd Continental Congress. Appointed Major General in June 1775, he was to lead the invasion of Canada. Ill health forced him to give the command over to someone else. Unfortunately for General Schuyler, the expedition was unsuccessful and he was dismissed in 1777.

Schuyler was a member of the Continental Congress and later served as a senator from New York for 4 years.

Burgoyne's Surrender by American painter John Trumball
(General Schuyler is 3rd from the left.)

General Schuyler's son-in-law was Alexander Hamilton. Together, along with John Jay and other Federalists, they led the movement in New York to ratify the Federal Constitution.

The *General Schuyler* was a small sloop purchased by the New York Committee of Safety in 1776. During the war, she operated in Long Island Sound and the Hudson River recapturing vessels that had been taken by the British.

The Bald Eagle's white head and tail feathers don't appear until the bird is three years old.

The use of the **bald eagle** as the symbol of the new nation began at the time of the establishment of the Great Seal of the United States in 1782. The eagle was chosen for its strength, effortless flight of freedom, long life, and also because it was thought to exist only on the American continent. The *Journals of Continental Congress* states: "The escutcheon (shield) is borne on the breast of an American Eagle without any other supporters, to denote that the United States of America ought to rely on their own virtue." The text notes that, "White signifies purity and innocence. Red, hardiness and valour and blue, the colour of the Chief, signifies vigilance, perseverance, and justice." In 1787, the American Bald Eagle was officially adopted as the national bird and emblem of the United States.

Benjamin Franklin and naturalist John James Audubon, however, thought that other qualities of the eagle made it an inappropriate symbol for America. Franklin thought the eagle's nasty habit of taking fish from other birds and its seeming retreat from smaller birds made it more a symbol of dishonesty and even cowardice. Franklin went on to claim that America's native bird, the turkey would be a better symbol, for at least it was a *courageous* bird!

The word "bald" does not mean the eagle has no feathers. Instead, it comes from the old word *piebald*, which means "marked with white."

Of all the game birds, only the wild turkey, grouse, and quail are native to the North American continent.

I ♥ acorns, fruit and seeds

Think I need a shave?

Male turkeys have a cluster of hair-like feathers called a "beard." Usually about 9" in length, some as long as 18 inches have been recorded.

melegris gallopavo

The Great Seal

Learn more about the Great Seal while you're coloring your own in the activity pages of this book.

is for our Flag* that makes us so proud.

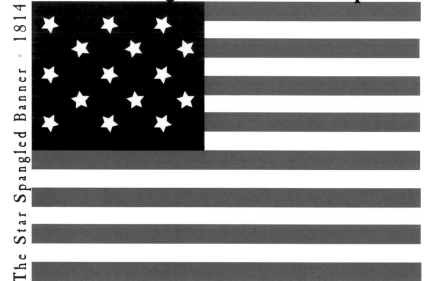

The Star Spangled Banner · 1814

FLAG • An ensign or colors; a cloth on which are usually painted or wrought certain figures and borne on a staff. In the army, a banner by which one regiment is distinguished from another.

✝ ..."Raise a banner for the nations."
Isaiah 62:10

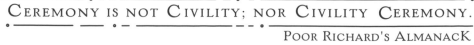

CEREMONY IS NOT CIVILITY; NOR CIVILITY CEREMONY.
POOR RICHARD'S ALMANACK

The Battle of Baltimore · September 12-14, 1814

On the morning of September 14, 1814, two hours after the bombardment had ended, the Star Spangled Banner was hoisted over the ramparts while the fife and drums played *Yankee Doodle.*

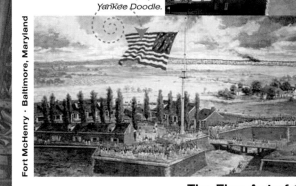

Fort McHenry · Baltimore, Maryland

The Flag Act of 1818

"The flag of the United States will be 13 horizontal stripes, alternated & white...with the admission of every state, one star will be added to the union."

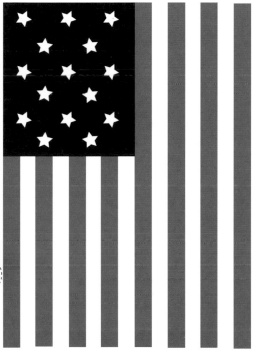

Why was Francis Scott Key on a British ship?

During the Battle of Baltimore, Key was on a "truce" ship to negotiate the release of his friend, who had been taken prisoner by the British. His vessel was 8 miles below Fort McHenry. As Key watched the attack, he penned his now famous poem, *"The Defence of Fort McHenry,"* later retitled, **"The Star Spangled Banner."**

Francis Scott Key

The music of the **"Star Spangled Banner"** had already been written in 1775 or 1776 by British composer John Stafford Smith. Francis Scott Key suggested his poem be sung to the tune of a well-known English drinking song, "To Anacreon in Heaven."

Anacreon or Ανακρεον was a Greek lyric poet born in 570 BC who was known for his drinking songs and hymns. Horace was one of his biggest fans.

GEE, WHERE'S BALTIMORE?

It was not until March 3, 1931, that President Herbert Hoover signed the law that designated the **"Star Spangled Banner"** as the U.S. National Anthem.

Each star is 2 feet across... each stripe, 2 feet wide.

You're in the Army now...

In 1812, the U.S. Infantry required those who enlisted to be able-bodied, 18-40 year-old men at least 5'6" tall who were free of "fits, ruptures, scurvy and habitual drunkenness." Their monthly pay was $8 and they were expected to serve for 5 years or until the war ended. At the war's end, they were rewarded with a land bounty of 160 acres in the territories of Michigan, Illinois, Louisiana or Maine.

"A" is for Armistead, the name of the family who cared for the flag for 3 generations. (Fort McHenry was once under the command of Gen. Armistead.) Eight feet of the original flag were cut off years ago. Parts were given to important people or soldiers who fought at the fort.

The 15 striped, 15 starred "Star Spangled Banner" can be seen at the Smithsonian Institution in Washington, D.C.

Color your own "Old Glory" and learn how to properly fold the flag in the activity pages at the back of this book.

Mary Pickersgill

Claggetts Brewery

In the summer of 1813, Mary Pickersgill, a professional flag maker living in Baltimore, was commissioned to make two flags for Fort McHenry. For the larger of the two (30' x 42'), she was paid $405.90. She bought 400 yards of English woolen bunting to make the stripes and union. The stars were made of cotton. She started the work with the help of her two daughters in her home, but when she needed to sew on the 15 stars, there was not enough room. A nearby brewery, *Claggetts*, let her use their maltroom to finish the work. The whereabouts of the smaller flag, a storm flag (17' x 25'), are unknown.

is for God*- to our motto be true.

New England Liberty Tree Flag • 1775

LIBERTY TREE

AN APPEAL TO GOD

*God · The Supreme Being; Jehovah; the eternal and infinite Spirit; the Creator, and the Sovereign of the Universe.

❋ *"Some trust in chariots and some in horses, but we trust in the name of the Lord our God."* Psalm 20:7

HOW MANY OBSERVE CHRIST'S BIRTHDAY; HOW FEW HIS PRECEPTS! O 'TIS EASIER TO KEEP HOLIDAYS THAN COMMANDMENTS.

POOR RICHARD'S ALMANACK

19

The first act of the Continental Congress was to request a session of prayer. Although there was dissent because several denominations were present, Sam Adams rose and claimed he could hear a prayer from *any* gentleman of piety and virtue as long as he was a patriot. The Rev. Duché (an Episcopalian) was selected. He read Psalm 35 to the delegates from the *Anglican Book of Common Prayer.*

Plead my cause, O Lord with them that strive with me. Fight against them that fight against me… Let those be turned back and humiliated who devise evil against me. " Psalm 35:1

"In God we trust…"

The national motto, "*In God we trust,*" first appeared on the 1864 two-cent coin. It was President Lincoln's last act signed into law before his death. It first appeared on paper currency in 1957.

Who's on…?

a. a $500 bill?

b. a $1,000 bill?

c. a $5,000 bill?

d. a $10,00 bill?

Salmon Chase

James Madison

Grover Cleveland

William McKinley

d.   c.   b.   a.

Annuit Coeptis??
That's Latin for "He has smiled on our undertakings."

The Eye of Providence or the All-Seeing Eye of God is inside a triangle. That's a symbol of the Trinity: Father, Son, and Holy Spirit.

ANNUIT COEPTIS
MDCCLXXVI
NOVUS ORDO SECLORUM

This is Latin, too. It means the "new order of the ages."

Great Seal side 2

Learn more about the Great Seal as you color your own on the activity pages in the back of this book.

Some Names of God used by George Washington: Jehovah, Superintending Providence, Power, Great Governor of the Universe, Divine Author of Our Blessed Religion, Almighty God, Giver of Life, Lord and Ruler of Nations, Creator, Maker, Great and Glorious Being, God of Armies, Deity, Supreme Judge of the World.

Did you know…? You'll see both sides of the Great Seal on the back of the dollar bill!

✝ + ✕ = ✳
greek cross or equilateral cross
chi cross (from the first letter of the word "Christ" in Greek)
called the Chi & Greek Cross

Did you know…?
One Nation under God
…in our *Pledge of Allegiance* comes from Lincoln's *Gettysburg Address.* "Under God" was added to the *Pledge* in 1954 under President Eisenhower to acknowledge America's heritage of faith in contrast to the godlessness of Communism.

Who was Salmon Chase?
Salmon Chase was the Secretary of the Treasury from 1861-1864. He oversaw the creation of the Federal Bureau of Engraving and Printing. In 1864 he was named Chief Justice of the Supreme Court.

ooo…I just LOVE his name! ♥
(oncorhynchus kisutch (coho or silver salmon))

Colonists originally used English, Spanish and French money. In 1775, the Continental Congress authorized the issuance of currency to finance the war effort. The threat of counterfeiting by the British was constant. To thwart these attempts, Ben Franklin used bits of mica (a shiny mineral) and leaf imprints when he printed this "Continental Currency." Backed only by a promise of tax revenues upon victory, the money quickly devalued which led to a popular expression, "not worth a Continental."

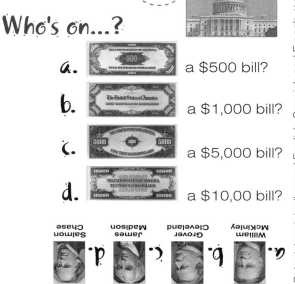

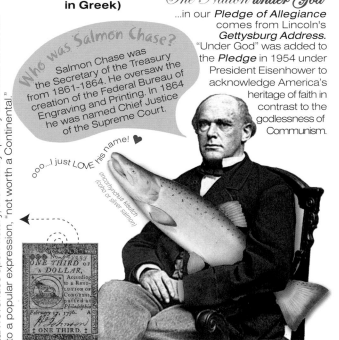

H is for Happiness that we can pursue.

Flag of the First Troop, Philadelphia Light Horse • 1774

FOR THESE WE STRIVE

Happiness • The agreeable sensations which spring from the enjoyment of good.

"All the days of the oppressed are wretched, but the cheerful heart has a continuous feast." Proverbs 15:15

VIRTUE & HAPPINESS ARE MOTHER AND DAUGHTER.

POOR RICHARD'S ALMANACK

THE FIRST TROOP PHILADELPHIA CITY CAVALRY

Captain Abraham Markoe gave this flag to the troops in 1775. For many years, it was believed to be the earliest flag of stripes in the United States. It has been discovered that the stripes were added over the existing Union Jack *canton*. It shows a Continental masquerading as a Native American holding a staff with a a *liberty cap* and a trumpeting angel symbolizing liberty and fame.

They call us now the 1st Squadron, 104th Cavalry Regiment in the PA National Guard.

DO YOU KNOW YOUR STANDARD FLAG AREAS?

H O I S T

CANTON

F L Y

WIDTH

LENGTH

So...what's a canton?

A canton is a type of flag that has a rectangular inset on the upper hoist side, the side by the flagpole.)

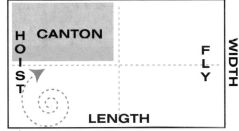

---- PILEUS
(or liberty cap)

It's a closefitting, brimless cap worn by the ancient Romans, copied from the Greek sailor cap called the *pilos*. It was worn by commoners or freed slaves. It regained popularity during the Renaissance in Italy (popular colors were black and red) and then again during the American and French Revolutions. It is sometimes represented on a spear or "liberty pole," a tall flagstaff planted in the ground.

Doing maneuvers on a Philadelphia street

The First Troop Philadelphia City Cavalry, founded in November 1774, is the oldest mounted military unit. It is still an active troop. Its members served as General George Washington's bodyguard and also fought in the Battles of Trenton, Princeton, Brandywine, and Germantown.

Carpenter's Hall

On Nov. 17, 1774, three members of Philadelphia's Safety Committee met in Carpenter's Hall with 25 leading citizens to form the cavalry troop of volunteers.

"Virtue is simply happiness..."
William Burroughs

The virtues intended by our Founders are clearly indicated by the 3 colors selected for the shield on the Great Seal. They are the same colors of the American Flag. "White signifies purity and innocence, **Red** hardiness and valor and **Blue** the colour of the Chief signifies vigilance, perseverance, and justice."

Learn more and color your own seal on the activity pages in the back of this book.

is for Independence,* self-government's new.

The Bennington Flag • 1777

76

*Independence • A state of being not dependent; complete exemption from control, or the power of others.

"Then you will know the truth, and the truth shall set you free."
John 8:32

IF YOU'D HAVE A SERVANT THAT YOU LIKE, SERVE YOURSELF.

POOR RICHARD'S ALMANACK

Independence Hall

Constructed between 1732 and 1756 as the State House of the Province of Pennsylvania, Independence Hall is considered a fine example of Georgian architecture. From 1775 to 1783, it was the meeting place for the Continental Congress. It was in the Assembly Room of this building that George Washington was appointed commander in chief of the Continental Army in 1775, and in this same room, the *Declaration of Independence* was adopted on July 4, 1776. It was also in the same room that the design of the American flag was agreed upon in 1777, the Articles of Confederation were adopted in 1781, and the U. S. Constitution was drafted in 1787.

Andrew Hamilton (amateur architect) and Edward Wooley (master builder) are credited with the design and construction of Independence Hall.

The days were VERY hot during the summer of 1787, and yet the windows of Independence Hall remained tightly shut. The Constitutional delegates wanted no one to overhear their discussions.

Made by John Folwell 1779

George Washington sat here.

The mahogany "rising sun" chair was used by George Washington for nearly three months as he presided over the Constitutional Convention.

" I have often looked at that chair behind the President without being able to tell whether it was rising or setting. But now I ...know it is a rising sun."

BENJAMIN FRANKLIN TO JAMES MADISON

The basement of Independence Hall was once used as Philadelphia's city dog pound.

...and they call this Independence Hall!??

Vermont's name comes from the French words *vert* (green) and *mont* (mountain). Vermont's nickname is "The Green Mountain State." In 1777, Vermont was declared an independent republic. It minted its own coins and had its own postal service. It was admitted to the Union in 1791, the first state to join the original 13.

Vermont

OOPS!
The Battle of Bennington did **NOT** take place in Bennington, but several miles west in a village called Walloomsac, New York.

★ Bennington

When farmer Reuben Stebbins heard the firing at the Battle of Bennington, he got out his horse and musket and headed for the battle to see *"who's goin' to own this farm."*

It's got six-pointed stars

This is the flag that flew at the Battle of Bennington, Vermont

"Vermont has to contain the most rebellious race on the continent..."

The Battle of Bennington by Chappel.

In the summer of 1777, General John Burgoyne successfully marched south from Lake Champlain down the Hudson River, easily capturing several forts along the way. By August, with his troops desperately needing food, wagons, cattle, and horses, Burgoyne decided that Bennington, a place where the patriots were storing supplies, was a great place to forage.
BAD MOVE!
On August 16, the 800 British, German, Loyalist, and Indian troops were met by 1600 patriots, organized by Ethan Allen and Seth Warner of "Green Mountain Boys" fame. They came from neighboring farms and militia. When the battle was over, 200 British troops had been killed and 700 taken prisoner. The victory was a tremendous morale booster for the newly formed Continental Army.

Gen. John Burgoyne
After losing the battle, a frustrated Burgoyne was heard to say...

J is for Justice* so each gets his due.

The New York State Flag, based on a 1777 flag, adopted in 1901

EXCELSIOR

* **JUSTICE** • The virtue which consists of giving to everyone what is his due; practical conformity to the laws and to principles of rectitude in the dealings of men with each other; honesty; integrity in commerce or mutual intercourse.

"When justice is done, it brings joy to the righteous but terror to evildoers."
Proverbs 21:15

PARDONING THE BAD IS INJURING THE GOOD.

POOR RICHARD'S ALMANACK

The first meeting of the U.S. Supreme Court was held on the second floor of The Royal Exchange in New York City, February 1, 1790. Due to transportation problems, only 3 of the 6 justices were present. Chief Justice John Jay adjourned the court until the next day. With an assembled quorum, they appointed a town crier and a clerk to admit lawyers to the Bar.

The Court moved to Philadelphia the next year, when it became the new national capitol, joining the rest of the federal government that was already there. The justices met in the East Wing of City Hall while Congress met in the West Wing. The new justices heard and decided their first actual case in 1792.

In 1800, the federal government moved permanently to Washington, D.C. As there was no place for the Court, Congress allowed it a room in the Capitol. From 1810-1860, the Court was held in the Old North Wing and later in the basement under the Senate Chamber. In 1912, William Howard Taft started lobbying for a separate building for the Court. When he was named Chief Justice in 1921, he redoubled his efforts. He died two years before the cornerstone of the new courthouse was laid in 1932.

When William Howard Taft became president (1909-1913), a larger bathtub needed to be installed in the White House to accommodate his ample 300-pound frame.

President W. H. Taft

The Seal of the Supreme Court is the same as the Great Seal.

THE SUPREME COURT OF THE U.S.

Each column is 30 feet tall and was constructed in 3 parts. They are 11 feet in circumference at the widest point.

It took 1,000 freight cars loaded with marble from Vermont to face the outside walls of the courthouse.

Cass Gilbert

Architect Cass Gilbert submitted his design for the Court building in 1929. He died in 1934, never living to see its completion a year later.

EQUAL JUSTICE UNDER LAW

Not everyone was enthusiastic about the new building for the court. Associate Justice Harlan Fiske Stone, commenting in 1935, said that he imagined the 9 justices would look like...

" ...NINE BLACK BEETLES IN THE TEMPLE OF KARNAK."

Did you know?...
Before they were appointed justices...

Justice Samuel Miller was a practicing physician. He received his M.D. in 1838 and practiced medicine in Kentucky until he was admitted to the Bar in 1847.

Justice Bryon R. White led the NFL in rushing while playing for Pittsburgh.

Justice Abe Fortas played violin with a jazz combo while in college in Tennessee.

The Highest Court in the Land!

SHHHHH.....

Did you know that directly above the courtroom where cases are heard is a full-sized basketball court? There's a sign warning that it should not be used when court is in session.

Lady of Justice

The origin of Lady Justice is probably the Greek goddess, *Themis*. Like the Roman goddess, *Justitia*, she was depicted wearing a blindfold and carried a sword and scale. She has come to represent the fair and equal administration of the law without corruption, avarice, prejudice or favor.

John Marshall

As a student at William & Mary College, Marshall studied philosophy under James Madison. From a successful law practice, he was elected to the Virginia House of Delegates and then later to the U.S. House of Representatives. In 1800, President John Adams appointed him Secretary of State. The next year he was appointed Chief Justice of the U.S. Supreme Court, where he served for 34 years.

During his tenure with the court, Marshall was primarily concerned with preserving private property rights, establishing the power and prestige of the court, and establishing a strong, central federal power.

is for Kings* without royalty.

IN MERIDIEM PROGRED ETC

*K I N G • The chief or sovereign of a nation; a man invested with supreme authority over a nation, tribe or country; a monarch. ━━━●❋●❋◍❋●❋●━━━

 "A large population is a king's glory, but without subjects a prince is ruined."

Proverbs 14:28

AN INNOCENT PLOWMAN IS MORE WORTHY THAN A VICIOUS PRINCE.

POOR RICHARD'S ALMANACK

King George III

George III is best known for two things: losing the American Colonies and going "mad." George III succeeded his grandfather, George II, in 1760. He became next in line after the death of his father, Frederick, nine years earlier. In 1761, he married Charlotte Mecklenburg-Strelitz from Germany, with whom he had 9 sons and 6 daughters.

George III was the third Hanoverian monarch. He was the first to be born in England and the first to speak English as his primary language. One of the most cultured kings, he started a collection of books (65,000 volumes) which later were given to the British Museum. He was the first royal to study science and had his own astronomical observatory. Avidly interested in agriculture, he was nicknamed "Farmer George," as he worked in the gardens at Richmond and Windsor.

George III was given bad political advice and for years had confusing and contradictory policies toward the American Colonies. Had King George shown interest in the grievances of the colonists earlier, war might have been avoided.

Afflicted with *porphyria,* George's health slowly deteriorated. Several attacks left him losing his grip on reality. At one state occasion, he rose and addressed the crowd, "My Lords and Peacocks..." Those who did not like him laughed; those who loved him cried. Soon after, his eldest son, George IV, was given the Crown. From 1811-1820, George III stayed at Windsor Castle attended by his doctors, confined in a straitjacket. He was deaf and blind when he died at age 82. He had reigned 60 years, the second longest rule in British history.

❓ Who had the longest reign in British history?

Queen Victoria reigned from 1837-1901...64 years!

The Carolina colony named a county (Mecklenburg) and a city (Charlotte) in the queen's name in hopes they'd gain favor from the Crown. Even today Charlotte is called "The Queen's City."

Devoted to his wife, George bought her *"The Queen's House."* Later enlarged, it became known as Buckingham Palace.

The onset of *Porphyria,* a genetic disorder, was first evident in George III just 5 years after he ascended the throne. Attacks, which included stomach aches and seizures, plagued the monarch throughout his rule until he was left deaf, blind, and insane. Sadly, his son George IV, who succeeded him, suffered from the same ailment.

Georgetown, D.C. was NOT named after George III but his grandfather, George II.

Charlotte Mecklenburg-Strelitz

Charlotte

What is Porphyria?

CHARLES I

I'm now a symbol of tyranny!

Charles I was King of England from 1625-49. His reign was filled with conflict. His marriage to a French Roman Catholic aroused suspicions and conflict among the Scots. Civil War broke out in 1641 and Parliament reached an agreement with their Scottish counterparts. Charles stubbornly resisted, using force to prohibit the establishment of Presbyterianism in England. He was captured, tried and executed January 30, 1649.

WEBB'S REGIMENT

IN MERIDIEM PROGRED ETC.

Webb's Regiment was the name for the 7th Connecticut Regiment under Col. Charles Webb of Stamford. When George Washington reorganized the army in 1779, it was renamed the 19th Continental Regiment.

America was often represented by a woman dressed like a Native American. In Webb's flag, she is shown with a liberty cap, an "American" flag and a sword to decapitate an enemy. The enemy here is *tyranny*, represented by Charles I, who was beheaded in 1649. The Latin expression *In Meridiem Progred Etc.* is translated "move beyond high noon," referring to the time of day Charles was killed.

Just call me Mr. President.

Another King George?

As the fledgling country was experiencing the difficulties of a newly-formed government, dissatisfaction led some citizens to speak of reinstating a monarchy. An incredulous George Washington told a friend, **"What astounding changes are a few years capable of producing! I am told that even respectable characters speak of a monarchical form of government, without horror... How irrevocable and tremendous! What a triumph for our enemies to verify their predictions! What a triumph for the advocates of despotism to find that we are incapable of governing ourselves, and that systems, founded on the basis of equal liberty, are merely ideal and fallacious!"**

Nathan Hale

A graduate from Yale College at the age of 18, Nathan Hale was a teacher when the Revolutionary War broke out. He accepted a commission as a 1st Lieutenant in the 7th Connecticut Regiment under Col. Webb. He later received a captain's commission in the newly-formed 19th Continental Regiment. He volunteered to try to find out information behind enemy lines of the planned site of the British invasion of Manhattan Island. Hale pretending he was a schoolteacher, was unfortunately captured and sentenced to be hanged the next day by General Howe. He died courageously at age 21, telling his captors,

"I only regret that I have but one life to give to my country."

is for the Bell that's called Liberty.*

Taunton Flag • This town in Mass. raised its own flag in 1774

LIBERTY AND UNION

* LIBERTY • Freedom from restraint; the body is at LIBERTY when not confined; the will or mind is at liberty when not checked or controlled; a man enjoys liberty when no physical force operates to restrain his actions or volitions. ⬥⬥✦⬤✦⬥⬥

..."*Proclaim liberty throughout the land unto all the inhabitants thereof...*" *Leviticus 25:10*

NOTHING BRINGS MORE PAIN THAN TOO MUCH PLEASURE; NOTHING MORE BONDAGE THAN TOO MUCH LIBERTY.

POOR RICHARD'S ALMANACK

The message on the Liberty Bell is a Bible verse:
"Proclaim liberty throughout the land unto all the inhabitants thereof..."
LEVITICUS 25:10

The Liberty Bell was ordered in 1751 by the Pennsylvania Assembly to commemorate the 50th anniversary of William Penn's *Charter of Privileges.* This charter speaks of the liberties valued by all, including the right of religious freedom, Native Americans' rights, and Penn's revolutionary idea of an informed citizenry which would enact laws.

Though the bell arrived from England in 1752, it wasn't hung in the PA State House (presently called Independence Hall) until a year later. It cracked with its first stroke of the clapper! Local foundry workers, John Pass and John Stowe were given the bell to recast. They added 1.5 oz. of copper to make it less brittle and put their names - **Pass & Stowe** - on the front of the bell. When the bell was rehung 19 days later, no one was thrilled with its sound and the city fathers asked the original maker, White Chapel Foundry in England, to cast another one. The new English bell, called its *Sister Bell*, sounded no better and was later used as a clock bell to sound off the hours.

The yoke is made of slippery elm.

The Liberty Bell's strike note is E flat!

How much does the Liberty Bell weigh?

??? ???

2080 lbs.

The Liberty Bell was used to call the Pennsylvania Assembly together and summon people for special events and announcements. In 1777, when the British were occupying Philadelphia, the Liberty Bell and all other bells in the city were removed lest they be melted down and turned into cannons or musket balls. The Liberty Bell was safely stored under the floorboards of Zion Reformed Church in Allentown, PA. On July 8, 1776, back home in Philadelphia, it was rung to announce the first public reading of the **Declaration of Independence**. By 1846, a thin crack began to affect its sound. It was repaired and rang out for George Washington's birthday. That year it cracked again and has been silent ever since.

Whatever happened to Sister Bell?

St. Augustine Church

The White Chapel replacement bell was first used to toll the hours in the State House. In the 1820s, it was moved to Old St. Augustine Church in Philadelphia as a permanent loan. The church was burned during a riot in 1844. The damaged bell was recast, and now hangs atop Villanova University Chapel in Pennsylvania.

Villanova University Chapel

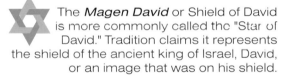

The *Magen David* or Shield of David is more commonly called the "Star of David." Tradition claims it represents the shield of the ancient king of Israel, David, or an image that was on his shield.

In the 17th century, it was popular to place this symbol on the outside of synagogues.

The symbol gained popularity as a symbol of Judaism during the Zionist movement in 1897, and is now on the flag of the State of Israel.

The **copperhead** is the most venomous snake found in the eastern United States. The colorfully patterned pit viper gets its name from the copper coloring on its head.

So who were the Loyal **9**?

Early in the summer of 1765, a group of **9** craftsmen and shopkeepers in Boston got together to oppose the Stamp Act. Dubbed the "Copperheads" by Samuel Adams, their numbers quickly increased to over 2,000, with members in every colony. Now called "The Sons of Liberty," they organized demonstrations, enforced boycotts, and became the American resistance through the time of independence.

the motto of the Sons of Liberty

"No taxation without representation"

Samuel Adams
1722-1803

His father owned a brewery.

A major leader in the War of Independence, Samuel Adams led the protest against the Stamp Act, founded The Sons of Liberty, helped to organize the Boston Tea Party, was a member of the Continental Congress, and signed the Declaration of Independence. His second cousin was John Adams, second president of the United States.

This was the flag of the Sons of Liberty, or *Liberty Flag,* which may have flown above the Liberty Tree, located at the corner of present day Washington and Essex Streets in downtown Boston. Its 7 red and 6 white bars represented the 13 original colonies.

The Sons of Liberty

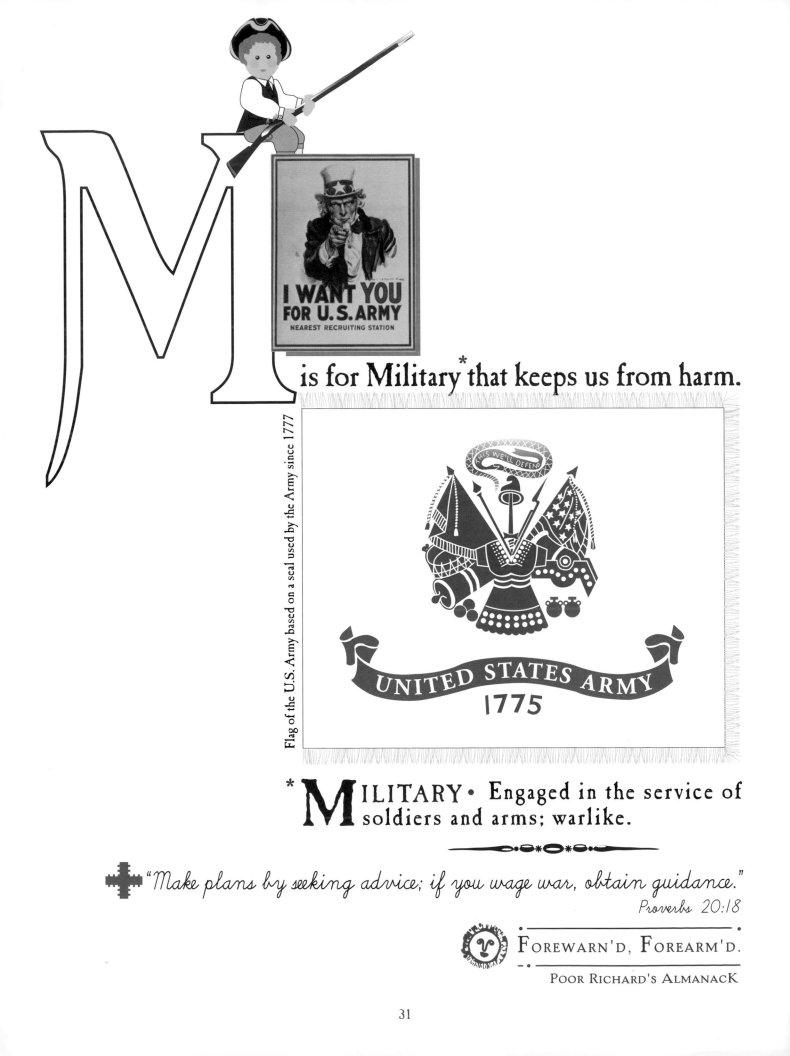

M

is for Military* that keeps us from harm.

Flag of the U.S. Army based on a seal used by the Army since 1777

I WANT YOU FOR U.S. ARMY
NEAREST RECRUITING STATION

THIS WE'LL DEFEND

UNITED STATES ARMY
1775

* **M**ILITARY • Engaged in the service of soldiers and arms; warlike.

"*Make plans by seeking advice; if you wage war, obtain guidance.*"
Proverbs 20:18

Forewarn'd, Forearm'd.

Poor Richard's Almanack

Timber Rattlesnake
crotalus horridus

"I hunt with fork-ed tongue!"

Indigenous to North America, the rattlesnake is a member of the pit viper family. Reaching lengths of 3-4.5 feet, pit vipers use heat sensitive areas in "pits" in the front of their heads to locate their victims, even in total darkness.

Contrary to popular opinion, a rattlesnake will not pursue or attack a person unless threatened or provoked. Its bite contains hemotoxin venom, which attacks the blood system of its prey.

Snakes with a complete set of rattles are rare. They usually break off.

The snake uses its tongue to "taste" the air and find its prey.

This is the first known political cartoon in an American newspaper (1758). The woodcut was drawn, cut, and published by Ben Franklin.

Note that Delaware and Georgia are missing. Delaware was still part of Pennsylvania at this time. It declared independence from both Great Britain and Pennsylvania in the same year, 1776.

What's a Jack?
...a flag hoisted at the bow of a ship. It identifies nationality but is not the same design as the ensign, or national flag.

DONT TREAD ON ME

JOIN, or DIE.

The sections of the snake represented the individual colonies and the curves signify the Atlantic coastline. New England was combined to form the head. The slogan *"Join or Die"* had nothing to do with Great Britain but was an urging to unify during the French and Indian War. At the time, superstition claimed that a snake cut in pieces would come back to life if one joined the sections together before sunset.

The Navy Jack
In the fall of 1775, the first ships of the Continental Navy were flying the Navy Jack, following the direction of Commodore Esek Hopkins. Jack flags had been used in the Royal Navy since the 15th century. The 13 stripes (for the colonies) and rattlesnake (a sign of resistance to Britain) symbolized the Revolutionary Era well.

Franklin's drawing reappeared in 1774, when Paul Revere updated it and added it to the masthead of the *Massachusetts Spy* showing a snake fighting a British dragon.

By 1775, the snake wasn't just in newspapers. It appeared all over the colonies on uniform buttons, paper money, banners, and flags. No longer a serpent, it was now the timber rattlesnake.

The Gadsden Flag • 1776

As a member of the Continental Congress, Christopher Gadsden helped to select Esek Hopkins the first Commander of the Navy. Tradition says that Gadsden presented him the yellow standard with snake as well as giving one to the Congress of his home state, South Carolina.

DON'T TREAD ON ME

In December 1775, an article was anonymously published in *An American Guesser*. (Most scholars agree it was written by Ben Franklin.) "The rattlesnake is found in no other place than America." It has sharp eyes and "may therefore be esteemed an emblem of vigilance...She never begins an attack, nor...ever surrenders. She is therefore an emblem of magnanimity and true courage...she never wounds 'til she has generously given notice, even to her enemy...one of the rattles singly is incapable of producing sound, but the ringing of the thirteen together is sufficient to alarm the boldest man living."

Who was Christopher Gadsden?

Born in Charleston, South Carolina in 1724, Gadsden was educated in England. A successful businessman, he became the leader of the SC Sons of Liberty. In 1776, he became a lieutenant colonel and was actively involved in the defense of Charleston. After the war, he was elected as governor of South Carolina, but he declined due to his age and health. He died in 1805.

The Seal of the Department of the Army

In the center is a Roman *cuirass*, a symbol of strength and defense. A Phrygian cap, or liberty cap, is supported on a sword's point. Centered above the cap is a rattlesnake holding in its mouth a banner that says **"THIS WE'LL DEFEND."** The snake signifies the army's constant readiness to defend and preserve the United States and our liberty.

Santa Fe ★

Arizona

New Mexico

★ Phoenix

Alamogordo

Yuma

Tucson

Las Cruces

Sierra Vista

The Gadsden Purchase

✳ CUIRASS ✳
(pronounced "kwi -ras")
The word's origin is French. It is body armor, an armored breastplate used in Roman and Medieval times.

The rattlesnake appeared on the $20 bill from Georgia dated 1778. The financial backing used for this currency was from property that had been seized from loyalists. The motto, *Nemo me impune lacesset,* is translated, "No one will provoke with impunity."

The grandson of Christopher Gadsden, James Gadsden, was appointed by President Franklin Pierce as U.S. Minister to Mexico. He was asked to broker a land deal so a railroad could be built to the Gulf of California. The treaty, signed by Gadsden and General Antonio López de Santa Anna, president of Mexico in 1853, ceded the 29,000 square miles of land located in southwestern New Mexico and southern Arizona and cost the U.S. $10 million.

 **N** is for Nature,* our forests and farms.

Flag of American Defense • Regimental Standard of 1778

THIS IS MINE & I WILL DEFEND IT!

* **N**ATURE · The physical universe; all things that are not made by people. The mountains, the forests, and the oceans are some of the wonders of nature. ——◦◦✦◦✦◦◦——

✠ *"He causes the grass to grow for the cattle, and herb for the service of man, that he may bring forth food out of the earth."* Psalm 104:14

 PLOUGH DEEP WHILE SLUGGARDS SLEEP; AND YOU SHALL HAVE CORN TO SELL AND KEEP.

POOR RICHARD'S ALMANACK

"Besides the advantages of liberty and the most equal constitution, heaven has given us a country with every variety of climate and soil, pouring forth in abundance whatever is necessary for the support, comfort and strength of a nation."

John Adams, August 1, 1776
Speech to the Continental Congress

John Adams was a Harvard-educated lawyer, active in the cause for independence. A signer of the *Declaration of Independence*, he was selected to be a delegate from Massachusetts for both the First and Second Continental Congresses. During the war, Adams was a diplomat to France and Holland. Later he served as vice president for George Washington. Unhappy with his new job, he complained to his wife, calling it "the most insignificant office that ever the invention of man confirmed or his imagination conceived." Happily, Adams later became president but for only one term for he was defeated by Thomas Jefferson in 1801. Adams died July 4, 1826, 50 years after signing the *Declaration*. Sighing his last words, "Thomas Jefferson still lives," he did not know that Jefferson had died only a few hours earlier.

John Adams

Who was John Josselyn?

Born in Essex, England, Josselyn traveled throughout New England during 1637-8 while visiting his Puritan brother. As he traveled, he observed and drew the flora and fauna of the New World. So complete were his observations that, upon his return to England, he published two works: **New-England's Rarities Discovered** (1672) and **An Account of Two Voyages to New-England** (1674), which remained the most authoritative writings on American natural science for more than a century.

Mountain Beaver • J.J. Audubon

Hey...watch out! Here comes that Josselyn guy!

Hollow Leafed Lavender drawn in the style of John Josselyn

Many believe that Josselyn might have been a physician, for he often wrote of the "excellent medicines" found here. "Beaver-glands" were apparently great for "Wind in the Stomach and Belly."

John Bartram
Father of American Botany

Orphaned at 13, John Bartram received little formal education. He taught himself botany, medicine, and surgery while working as a farmer. With his fifth child, William, Bartram traveled north to Lake Ontario, west to the Ohio River and south to Florida, searching and collecting specimens for his own garden and for collectors worldwide. By 1765, he had developed so fine a reputation for his knowledge of plants that George III named him Royal Botanist. Along with his lifelong friend Ben Franklin, Bartram formed the American Philosophical Society.

John Bartram's family garden, America's first botanical garden, is still open to the public in Philadelphia.

WILLIAM BARTRAM

While on an expedition through North Carolina, South Carolina and Georgia in 1765, naturalist and artist William Bartram discovered a flowering tree along the Alatahama River. He named it *franklinia alatahama* after his father's friend, Benjamin Franklin. He published a record of his journey in 1791 called *Travels*.

Alexander Wilson, first to paint all the known birds of America

The "Father of American Ornithology," Wilson was a weaver by trade. He left his native Scotland for the freedoms promised in the *Declaration of Independence*. He moved near to the Bartram family, where he and William Bartram became good friends. Recognizing his artistic ability, Bartram asked him to draw some of their garden's specimens. Later, Wilson wrote to Thomas Jefferson requesting to be included in his expedition to explore the West. His letter arrived too late, but in the years that followed, the two became good friends. His book, *Wilson's American Ornithology*, was published in 10 volumes in 1813. Wilson died before it was released.

franklinia alatahama

The travels of Meriwether Lewis and William Clark
were officially called "Corps of Volunteers on a Expedition of North Western Discovery"

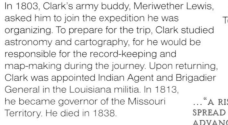
British Possessions
Fort Clatsop
Oregon Country
Indiana Territory
St. Louis
Spanish Possessions
Louisiana Territory

An army veteran, 29-year-old Capt. Lewis was Jefferson's private secretary prior to the trip. Visiting Philadelphia before he left, Lewis studied under Andrew Ellicot (astronomy), Benjamin Rush (medicine), Caspar Wistar (anatomy) and Benjamin Barton (botany). When he returned from the expedition in 1806, he was named governor of the Louisiana Territory. On Oct. 11, 1809, he died on his way to Washington from St. Louis.

Meriwether Lewis

Chow time!
When game was abundant, each man on the expedition ate about **9 pounds of meat** each day!

In 1803, Clark's army buddy, Meriwether Lewis, asked him to join the expedition he was organizing. To prepare for the trip, Clark studied astronomy and cartography, for he would be responsible for the record-keeping and map-making during the journey. Upon returning, Clark was appointed Indian Agent and Brigadier General in the Louisiana militia. In 1813, he became governor of the Missouri Territory. He died in 1838.

William Clark

Lewis' telescope

..."A RISING NATION, SPREAD OVER A WIDE AND FRUITFUL LAND, ADVANCING RAPIDLY TO DESTINIES BEYOND THE REACH OF THE MORTAL EYE."
Thomas Jefferson's First Inaugural Speech

Jefferson originally talked to George Rogers Clark about a trip westward. Clark, a former neighbor in Virginia, had sent him shells, tusks, seeds and bones that he had found in his new home, Kentucky. Jefferson grew concerned that the British were raising money for explorers and he wanted to beat them to it. Clark declined the offer and instead recommended his younger brother, William, who also knew the Indian territory. Two years after he was elected president, Jefferson asked Congress for $2,500 to finance an expedition. In 1804, Jefferson sent Meriwether Lewis and William Clark to find a waterway to the Pacific and to explore the uncharted West. It took them and 38 others 2 years, 4 months and 10 days to travel 8,000 miles. Remarkably, only one man, Sgt. Charles Floyd, died on the way - of appendicitis.

is for Opinions that we're free to say.*

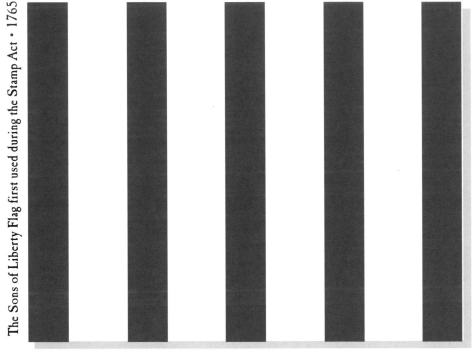

OPINION · The judgment which the mind forms of any proposition, statement, theory or event, the truth or falsehood of which is supported by a degree of evidence that renders it probable, but does not produce absolute knowledge or certainty.

✠ *"Reckless words pierce like a sword, but the tongue of the wise brings healing."*
Proverbs 12:18

 TART WORDS MAKE NO FRIENDS: A SPOONFUL OF HONEY WILL CATCH MORE FLIES THAN A GALLON OF VINEGAR.

POOR RICHARD'S ALMANACK

"Our opinions do not really bloom into fruition until we express them to someone else."

Mark Twain

BORN: JANUARY 28, 1737 • DIED: JUNE 8, 1809

"These are the times that try men's souls."

THOMAS PAINE

More than 500,000 copies sold!

"COMMON SENSE:"

the pamphlet penned by Thomas Paine in January 1776. In it he expressed that the colonies had the right to revolt against a government which imposed taxes without representation. In Paine's **opinion**, it was just *"common sense"* to stop recognizing *"the big brute,"* George III.

Born in England, the son of a Quaker corset maker, Thomas Paine was a failure at most of what he tried. He failed at school, worked for his father, went to sea, and worked as an excise officer. Each time he found himself dismissed: In London in 1774, he happened to meet Benjamin Franklin, who encouraged him to come to America. Later that year, he arrived in Philadelphia and began his new life as a journalist by publishing a treatise against slavery in America. Two years later, he wrote **Common Sense,** which helped light the flames of revolution in the hearts of the colonists. Paine served unsuccessfully as a soldier. After the war, he returned to Europe where he wrote a piece against the monarchy which inflamed the British. He fled England to avoid arrest. In France, a country embroiled in its own revolution, Paine was imprisoned for not supporting the execution of Louis XVI. There he began writing **The Age of Reason**, the work in which he expressed strongly anti-religious views.

Paine returned to the U.S. in 1802 to find that his contribution to the American Revolution had been forgotten, the result of his anti-religious views. "His name is enough," commented a peer. John Adams had first said that "history is to ascribe the American Revolution to Thomas Paine." Later, he called him "a disastrous meteor." Thomas Paine died at 72, forgotten and abandoned by his friends.

After his death, Paine's fall from grace was sung by children in this nursery rhyme.

Poor Tom Paine, there he lies:
Nobody laughs, and nobody cries,
Where he has gone or how he fares,
Nobody knows and nobody cares.

R.I.P.

Though the Republicans are called the "Grand Old Party," the Democrat Party was organized 22 years earlier

REPUBLICAN OR DEMOCRAT?

Political opinions in America are often represented by the political parties. The modern Democratic Party can trace its beginnings back to the 1820s and Andrew Jackson. The Republican Party won its first presidential victory in 1858 with the election of Abraham Lincoln.

As president, Andrew Jackson strengthened the office of the president by his exercise of his veto power. He was called "King Andrew I" by his foes.

THE GOP

The nickname comes from the 1870s. It stood for "Grand Old Party," coined from newspaper headlines from the *Boston Post* and *New York Herald.* In later years it stood for "Gallant Old Party," "Get Out and Push" (during early motoring days), the "GoParty," and "Generation of Peace."

Statesman, lawyer, and orator, Daniel Webster was considered the outstanding debater of his day.

Why a donkey or elephant?

The symbols for the two parties were products of the creative genius of Thomas Nast. Nast, considered America's most important political cartoonist, did most of his work for *Harper's Weekly*, the leading illustrated magazine of the late 19th century. His imagination also produced Santa images and Uncle Sam.

COPPERHEAD PRESS

"Git off yer soap box!"

Maltese Cross

Used by the Knights of Malta during the Crusades

Where's Malta?

It's an island in the Mediterranean, south of Italy. Legend says St. Paul was shipwrecked there.

FAIRBANK'S SANTA CLAUS SOAP — HANDIEST SHAPE — LASTS LONGEST

The first official Soap Box Derby was held on August 19, 1933, in Dayton, Ohio.

Soap was once delivered to stores in sturdy wooden crates. The old boxes were often reused as a portable "stage" for an orator to stand on so he could rise above the crowd to make speeches. Children also put wheels on them and made vehicles which raced in a "Soap Box Derby."

P is for Patriot, who pointed the way.

LIBERTY OR DEATH

PATRIOT • A person who loves his country, and zealously supports and defends it and its interests; devoted to the welfare of one's country.

"The memory of the righteous will be a blessing, but the name of the wicked will rot." Proverbs 10:7

IF YOU WOULD NOT BE FORGOTTEN, AS SOON AS YOU ARE DEAD AND ROTTEN, EITHER WRITE THINGS WORTH READING, OR DO THINGS WORTH THE WRITING.

POOR RICHARD'S ALMANACK

Φιλοπατρια???

Our word *patriotism* comes from the Greek word Φιλοπατρια or *philopatria.* It literally means "love of fatherland" or "love of country."

John Witherspoon

Born in Scotland in 1723, John Witherspoon was the son of a Presbyterian minister and a descendant of the Scottish reformer, John Knox. A diligent student, Witherspoon went to college at age 14, later receiving a Doctor of Divinity degree. While still living in Scotland he was approached by **Benjamin Rush** and **Richard Stockton** to become the next president of the College of New Jersey, now Princeton University. He agreed after his wife overcame her fear of the trans-Atlantic voyage and then went on to successfully lead the college into becoming a prestigious center of learning.

John Witherspoon was the only member of the clergy and the only college president to sign the Declaration of Independence. He also lost a son in the Revolutionary War.

Dr. Witherspoon was elected to the Continental Congress and signed the *Declaration of Independence*, along with Dr. Rush and Mr. Stockton. In November 1776, with the British approaching Princeton, he shut down and evacuated the college. The British troops nearly destroyed the school. After the war, Witherspoon devoted his life to restoring the damage. He also served twice in the N.J. State Legislature. In his later years, Dr. Witherspoon lost his sight and retired to his farm, "Tusculum," just outside Princeton, where he died in 1794.

John Witherspoon's influence on the fledgling nation of the United States was astounding. His students included a president and a vice president, 9 cabinet officers, 21 senators, 39 congressmen, 3 justices of the Supreme Court, and 12 state governors!

TUSCULUM... was an ancient city south of Rome. It was the favorite summer residence of Roman nobles and emperors.

Tusculum today

The Signers of the Declaration did so at great cost

- ★ Five signers were captured by British as traitors, tortured, then died.
- ★ Twelve had their homes ransacked and burned.
- ★ Two lost sons in the war; two had sons captured.
- ★ Nine of the 56 fought and died from wounds or hardship.

"America is the only vivid principle of the whole world."
Dr. Benjamin Rush

Richard Stockton | Dr. Benjamin Rush

Richard Stockton was once a respected scholar and lawyer and the first New Jersey delegate to sign the Declaration. Captured by Loyalists and imprisoned in New York, he was later released in poor health and found all his property had been destroyed. He died a pauper at age 51.

Delegate to the Continental Congress in 1775 and signer of the **Declaration**, Dr. Rush tended to the wounded at the battles of Trenton, Brandywine, Princeton, and Germantown and the sick at Valley Forge. He refused all compensation for his military service. After the war, he gained fame in medicine and as a tireless advocate for social causes: the abolition of slavery, treatment for the mentally ill, and for education for women and the poor.

A Patriotic Wedding

♥ Stockton's daughter, Julia, married Dr. Rush in 1776. She was 16...he was 30. In attendance were two signers of the Declaration. Rev. Witherspoon married the pair who later raised 13 children.

"ONE OF OUR MOST BAWLING DEMAGOGUES AND VOLUMINOUS WRITERS IS A CRAZY DOCTOR."
TORY PAMPHLETEER DESCRIBING DR. JOSEPH WARREN

Dr. Joseph Warren
Born: June 10, 1741
Died: June 17, 1775

Another physician played an historic role in our nation's early history. Harvard graduate Dr. Joseph Warren began his activities for freedom after the Stamp Act was enacted. The Massachusetts native developed a close friendship with Sam Adams and attended every town meeting after the British troops arrived in Boston. When hostilities broke out, Warren refused to serve his country as a physician, choosing instead to become an officer. His rank was Major General. As he was attempting to rally his troops near Bunker Hill, Dr. Warren became the first officer to be killed in the war when he was hit in the head by a musket ball.

When Dr. Warren died he left 4 children orphaned, as their mother had died 2 years earlier. They were struggling financially when General Benedict Arnold, an old friend of their father, came to their relief. He not only personally contributed money for their education but also convinced Congress to give them half the amount of a Major General's pay until they were "of age."

Benedict Arnold wasn't ALL bad!

The Hanover flag

This flag, with its vigilant patriot, was the standard for the **Hanover Associators** (another name for *volunteers*). The citizens of Hanover, Pennsylvania met on July 4, 1774 and adopted this flag and resolved: *"That in event of Great Britain attempting to force unjust laws upon us. By the strength of our arms, our cause we leave to Heaven and our rifles."*

PENNSYLVANIA

Where in the world is Hanover, PA? The borough of Hanover, named after the city in Germany, is located near the Maryland border in southeastern PA. Because it produces so many pretzels and potato chips, Hanover is now known as the "Snack Capital of the World."

Yum!

Q is for Queens,* who've lost their command.

BEWARE THE FATE OF BRITAIN

BRITANNIA

***Q**UEEN • A woman who is the sovereign of a kingdom.

✝ *"A wife of noble character is her husband's crown, but a disgraceful wife is like decay in his bones."* Proverbs 12:4

THE ROYAL CROWN CURES NOT THE HEAD-ACHE.

POOR RICHARD'S ALMANACK

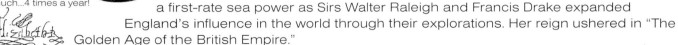

Regina is Latin for queen

Elizabeth Regina
"Good Queen Bess," "Gloriana," "The Virgin Queen"

Elizabeth was the daughter of Henry VIII and Anne Boleyn. Like her father she was a writer, a poet and fluent in a number of languages. Short-tempered and sometimes indecisive, Elizabeth relied on the advice of court councilors. During her reign of nearly 45 years, she successfully managed to keep the religious wars in check and fought back an advancing Spanish fleet. In a speech given before the battle of the Spanish Armada, Elizabeth exclaimed, "I know I have the body of a weak and feeble woman, but I have the heart and stomach of a king." Under her rule, England became a first-rate sea power as Sirs Walter Raleigh and Francis Drake expanded England's influence in the world through their explorations. Her reign ushered in "The Golden Age of the British Empire."

In Tudor times Elizabeth was considered strange for bathing so much...4 times a year!

Drake named his colony *Virginia* after the "Virgin Queen."

Aboard the Golden Hind, Drake became the first Englishman to sail around the world. The three year adventure prompted Elizabeth to knight him. He was appointed Vice-Admiral of the British Fleet before the battle with the Spanish Armada. His ventures made this son of a poor farmer/seaman the first English millionaire.

Sir Francis Drake

MEMOIRS
OF
MAJOR-GENERAL HEATH,
CONTAINING
ANECDOTES, DETAILS OF SKIRMISHES,
BATTLES, and other MILITARY EVENTS,
DURING THE
AMERICAN WAR.
WRITTEN BY HIMSELF.

What does this flag mean?

BEWARE THE FATE OF BRITAIN

In 1798, Gen. Heath published this book containing a history of the Revolution and sketched the flag at left. For more flags by General Heath, see the *Activity Pages*.

General William Heath was a farmer, soldier, and political leader from Massachusetts. As a brigadier general, he saw action at Lexington and Concord, New York City, Long Island, Harlem Heights, and White Plains. After the war, he helped his state ratify the *Constitution* in 1788, served as a state senator, and was elected lieutenant governor in 1800 (though he declined the office.) The flag he sketched in the journal he kept throughout the war shows a seated **Britannia** with shield, helmet, and cuirass (see letter M) weeping as she has seen the mast broken on her ship, symbolic of her empire. Atop the mast, the red cap of liberty (see letter L) is burning with flames of freedom.

young Walt

♥ I was one of the Queen's favorites... once, too. ♥

Although there is no confirmation that he spread his cloak for the queen to walk over a puddle, Sir Walter Raleigh had great charm and was a favorite of the court. He organized the expedition to colonize the New World. He was knighted and dubbed "Lord and Governor of Virginia."

Sir Walter Raleigh

Magna Britannia, The Colonies Reduced

In 1767, this card was distributed to members of Parliament by Benjamin Franklin, who was in England representing the colonies at the time. It was drawn (many believe by Franklin) to show the British the effects the Stamp Act had upon the colonies. It shows a dismembered Britannia whose limbs are labelled "Virg, Pennsyl-, New York and New Eng." The banner draping her in Latin states, *"Date Obolum BelliSario,"* or "Give a penny to Belisarius."

1st potato brought back to Europe was planted in Raleigh's Irish estate.

Rule Britannia?

Who is Belisarius? Once a great Roman general, **Belisarius** became sightless and was reduced to begging for food at the gates of Rome, crying, "Give one penny to poor Belisarius." Obviously, the colonies saw Britain as the hapless Belisarius.

Britannia was the Latin name given by the Romans to the southern part of Great Britain. Coins issued under Hadrian personified Britannia for the first time. During the Renaissance, the image of Britannia as a symbol of England was revived, appearing on a farthing from 1672 and later on this 1844 groat.

Since the Middle Ages, a groat is the name given to all thick silver coins.

Queen Henrietta Maria

Queen Christina of Sweden

Christina became queen of Sweden in 1632 when her father Gustav II died in battle. Six years later the first Swedes established a colony in the New World near present-day Wilmington, Delaware, and named it Fort Christiana.

THE CROSS OF ST. PETER

Legend says that when Peter was to be crucified by the Romans, he requested that his cross be placed downward, for he was not worthy to have died in the same way as his Lord.

MARYLAND

1609-1669
The State of Maryland received its name from the wife of Charles I, King of England and Ireland, who signed the 1634 charter establishing the colony. A devout Catholic, Queen Henrietta Maria survived her husband, who was beheaded in 1649. Their sons, Charles II and James II, ruled England from 1660-1688.

is for Republic, representatives rule in our land.

REPUBLIC • A commonwealth; a state in which the exercise of the sovereign power is lodged in representatives elected by the people.

✝ *"Plans fail for lack of counsel, but with many advisers they succeed."*
Proverbs 15:22

THE MAGISTRATE SHOULD OBEY THE LAWS, THE PEOPLE SHOULD OBEY THE MAGISTRATE.

POOR RICHARD'S ALMANACK

"A representative republic in which the people freely choose deputies to make laws for them, is much the best form of government hitherto invented."

"Federal Catechism," The American Spelling Book (Boston, 1798)

Noah Webster included the "Federal Catechism" in his widely used spelling book, teaching American students the differences in governments and the benefits of being ruled in a representative republic. Born in 1758, the son of a farmer/weaver, Webster loved learning and devoted his life to academic pursuits.

In 1783, Webster published *A Grammatical Institute of the English Language,* more commonly called "The Blue-backed Speller" because of its cover. It was in use for over 100 years. At age 43, he started writing a dictionary, using American spelling for the first time and including Native American words such as *skunk, squash, hickory, and chowder*. Twenty-seven years and 70,000 words later, it was finished. His dictionary has sold more copies than any English book other than the Bible.

Noah Webster

Webster thought spelling phonetically would make it easier for foreigners to learn our language, so he changed the spelling of certain words. But some of his suggestions never caught on like, *tung,* for "tongue" and *wimmen* for "women."

New American Spelling	Old English Spelling
plow	plough
center	centre
color	colour
music	musik

During his life, Webster mastered **20** languages including Chaldean, Syriac, Hebrew, Arabic, Ethiopic & Persian.

Who is it?

The figure on top of the Capitol dome is...

a. Lady Liberty
b. Columbia
c. Freedom

Sculptor Thomas Crawford designed the bronze statue in1855. It was originally to have a liberty cap, but Secretary of War Jefferson Davis objected and it was changed to a crested helmet. At the time the liberty cap was the symbol of freed slaves. Davis, the future President of the Confederacy, was pro-slavery.

The answer is "C."
Her complete name is "Freedom Triumphant in War and Peace."

LIBERTY
2ND CANADIAN

2ND CANADIAN REGIMENT "CONGRESS' OWN"

Also called **"Hazen's Regiment"** after commanding officer, Colonel Moses Hazen of Vermont, the 2nd Canadian Regiment was raised at large in 1776. Most of the men came from Canada and Pennsylvania. The men wore black leather caps and their uniforms were brown and white with facings. The Regimental Cipher "C.O.R." and the motto **"Pro Aris et Focis"** appeared on their drum, caps, and the canteens. It was independent of any state and was solely under the control of Congress. The Regiment fought valiantly at the battles of Brandywine, Yorktown and many others, but their work lives on today on the **Hazen Road.**

PRO ARIS ET FOCIS means "for our altars and our homes."

The Hazen Military Road This 48-mile road that traverses the Green Mountains was built between 1776-79 by soldiers and settlers who worked for $10 a month and a daily pint of rum. It was never used for its original intention to move troops from the Connecticut River to striking distance of Montreal, Cananda. Instead, it helped open up Vermont for settlement after the war.

CONGRESS

Derived from the middle English word *congresse*, or "body of attendants," the word originally came from the Latin word for "meeting." The Congress of the U.S. is the national legislative body that consists of the **Senate** and the **House of Representatives.**

Each 2-year term of the U.S. Congress is called a congress. Congresses are numbered consecutivelyfrom the first (1789-1791) to the current. Congress always begins on January 3rd and has two sessions.

The Constitutional Convention of 1787 determined how our representative government would work. There was heated disagreement over the make-up of the new national legislature. Edmond Randolph of Virginia suggested that the new body would have supreme powers over all matters on which separate states were not competent to act, as well as the power to veto any and all state laws. He also wanted at least one house of the legislature to be directly elected by the people. It became known as the *Virginia Plan.* Small states were afraid the larger states with their larger representation would consistently out-voted them. They wanted each state to have one vote. William Patterson of New Jersey, backed by Connecticut, New York, Delaware, and Maryland, proffered his idea, calling it the *New Jersey Plan.*

THE NEW JERSEY PLAN
I don't TRUST you!

Do I have a plan for YOU...
THE VIRGINIA PLAN

What is the... **ELECTORAL COLLEGE?**

The debate was so heated that Franklin asked that each day's meeting begin with a prayer.

BEN FRANKLIN
played a key role in offering a solution, called the **Great Compromise.** It provides for a legislature with two houses. **The House of Representatives** would consist of 65 members based on a state's population. The **Senate** would have 2 senators from each state to be chosen by the state's legislature. An **Electoral College** would choose the president. The first draft was approved by all 12 states present. (Rhode Island did not send a delegate.) Three delegates refused to sign, among them Edmond Randolph of Virginia.

At the Constitutional Convention some thought a purely popular election of the president was too reckless. Others objected to giving Congress the power. The establishment of the Electoral College was the compromise. Its members, or electors, equal the number of senators plus the number of U.S. Representatives from the state. This varies with the state's population. The electors meet in their state capitals the Monday following the 2nd Wednesday of December to officially cast their ballots.

S is for Stars* on a field of blue.

STAR • A luminous body in the heavens, that appears in the night, or when its light is not obscured by clouds or lost in the brighter radiance of the sun. Their immense numbers exhibit the astonishing extent of creation and of divine power.

"The light of the righteous shines brightly, but the lamp of the wicked is snuffed out." Proverbs 13:9

THE CONSTELLATION...DENOTES A NEW STATE TAKING ITS PLACE AND RANK AMONG OTHER POWERS.

CONTINENTAL CONGRESS, 1782

"The Flag of the united states be 13 stripes alternate red & white, that the union be 13 stars white in a blue field representing *a new constellation* ."

What's a Constellation?

→ a formation of stars perceived as a figure or pattern

Hey, there's *Nova Comstella!* (the New Constellation)

Quincuncial? ☞
Latin for "five" and "one" *quincuncial* means having the form of a *quincunx*. Old Glory's stars are based on a repetition of 5 units.

THIS IS A QUINCUNX

Just another starving artist!

Francis Hopkinson was a man of many talents. The first graduate of the University of Pennsylvania, Hopkinson went on to study law. He later became a Congressman from New Jersey, signer of the *Declaration of Independence*, poet, and artist...He was even once the organist at Christ Church in Philadelphia.

The design of the first "Stars and Stripes." created by Francis Hopkinson, had all13 of the 6-pointed stars in a staggered pattern, technically called "quincuncial." In a flag of 13 stars the placement produced the outline of the crosses of St. Andrew (✕) and St. George (✚).

The Journals of the Continental Congress show clearly that Francis Hopkinson designed the flag, but he was never paid for his work. Although he petitioned Congress several times, his request for "a quarter cask of the public wine" went unheeded. He was considered a public servant and thus ineligible to receive payment.

Fras Hopkinson

The Betsy Ross Flag is often thought of as the first American flag. Her descendants claimed she made (not designed) the first U.S. flag, using a circular arrangement of 5-pointed stars.
You can cut your own 5-pointed star when you go to the *Activity Pages* in the back of this book.

Hopkinson also helped design the Great Seal, in which he included another **constellation**. This one is found in the "cloud" above the eagle's head. *This* constellation symbolizes that "a new State is taking its place among the other nations."

13 stars stripes & arrows olive leaves for the 13 states

USS CONSTELLATION
37 USA
2004

The Great Seal was a product of 3 committees. In July 1776, the first committee (B. Franklin, Thomas Jefferson, & John Adams) asked artist Pierre Fugéne du Simitiére to help them with a design. A second committee was formed in March 1780 and asked Francis Hopkinson to draw up a sketch. In 1782, the final committee asked Charles Thomson who, by combining the elements from prior submissions with ideas of his own, created the design which ultimately became the Seal.

E PLURIBUS UNUM

original die of Seal (1782)

Thomson's final design

USS Constellation in Baltimore

Named after the **constellation of stars** on the American flag, the *USS Constellation* was launched in Baltimore on September 7, 1797. As the first frigate to be commissioned by the U.S. Navy, she saw action in the Caribbean and the Barbary States. During the War of 1812 she helped protect Norfolk, Virginia from the British. Although repaired and overhauled several times, by 1853 it was no longer cost-effective to keep her afloat. She was decommissioned and broken up in Portsmouth, Virginia.

A new ship named the *Constellation*, designed as a "sloop of war," was commissioned in 1855. She served as an anti-slaver, going to Africa to catch those engaged in the illegal slave trade. Active in the Civil War, she later brought food and supply relief to famine victims in Ireland. The *USS Constellation* was designated a "naval relic" in 1933. She was brought into dry-dock in Baltimore in 1954, where you can still see her today.

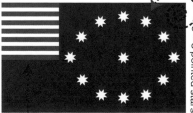

13 red & white stripes

13 – 8 pointed stars

Easton Flag
Legend has it that the Easton Flag was displayed for the reading of the *Declaration of Independence* on July 8, 1776, in Easton, Pennsylvania. Local people believe that the women of the town created the 55" x 97" flag by using grosgrain for the stripes on a field of India silk.

Easton is the home of Crayola crayons!

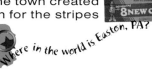
PENNSYLVANIA
Where in the world is Easton, PA?

44

 is for the Tree of Liberty,* from Boston it grew.

The Liberty Tree Flag • 1774

LIBERTY TREE

AN APPEAL TO GOD

*LIBERTY TREE • Following the example of the Sons of Liberty in Boston, patriots throughout the original colonies chose a tree, strong in stature, as a meeting place where they could discuss their grievances against the King and eventually make plans for independence. These trees represented the colonies' desire for self-rule and liberty, hence the name, "Liberty Tree."

"The fruit of the righteous is a tree of life, and he who wins souls is wise."
Proverbs 11:30

THE TREE OF LIBERTY MUST BE WATERED FROM TIME TO TIME WITH THE BLOOD OF PATRIOTS...

THOMAS JEFFERSON

"Let the far and near all unite with a cheer, in defense of our Liberty Tree."

Thomas Paine, *Pennsylvania Magazine*, July 1775

During 1765, the Sons of Liberty gathered under a large 120-year-old elm tree in Boston, Massachusetts to protest the Stamp Act, a much-hated tax imposed on the colonists for all published materials. They concluded the protest by "hanging in effigy" tax collectors from the tree. It was known from then as a **"Liberty Tree."** Soon, every colony had its own Liberty Tree. When the British chopped down the Boston tree and used it for firewood, colonists crafted flags using its image.

The cut down elm in Boston produced 14 cords of firewood. A cord of firewood is 128 cubic feet of wood, or a stack measuring 8' long by 4' wide by 4' tall.

Before and during the Revolutionary War, Liberty Trees in other cities experienced similar fates. In Charleston, South Carolina, the huge Live Oak, under which Christopher Gadsen began talking independence (See letter "M"), was cut down and burned when the British captured the city. Instead of a tree, New York City had a Liberty Pole, which was chopped down and re-erected three times...each time getting thicker and having more protection around it.

The last of the original Liberty Trees stood on the campus of St. John's College in Annapolis, Maryland. In 1999, the nearly 600-year-old, 96-foot tulip poplar was damaged by a hurricane. On October 25, 1999, the governor of Maryland and several hundred onlookers said good-bye. It took 4 days for workers to cut down the massive tree.

LAST STANDING LIBERTY TREE

The Sons of Liberty

A broadside (poster) posted by Boston's Sons of Liberty in 1770.

On the Death of Five young Men who was Murthered, *March* 5th 1770. By the 29th Regiment.

At first, the Sons of Liberty saw their role as organizers of protests against government policies rather than disrupting royal authority. The group waned after the repeal of the Stamp Act (1766) but became active again with the passage of the Townshend Act the next year. Its members were prominent up to the time of the First Continental Congress in 1774.

The original flag of the Sons of Liberty was 9 vertical stripes which represented **liberty poles**. It later grew to 13 stripes and shifted horizontally. Called the "rebellious stripes," it provided the inspiration for our present day flag.

What's a masthead?

Not just the head or top of a mast on a ship, a **masthead** is the title of a newspaper or magazine. It's usually printed on the front page and on the editorial page.

FAMOUS SON OF LIBERTY, PAUL REVERE

Paul Revere was born in December 1734, the son of Apollos Rivoire, a French Huguenot (Protestant) immigrant from whom he learned gold and silver-smithing. After his return from service in the French-Indian War, he married Sarah Orne and had 8 children. Sarah died in 1733, after the birth of their eighth child. Revere remarried the next year, and with Rachael Walker, had 8 more children.

He owned a silver shop for 40 years and, needing to supplement his income to provide for his large family, Revere made engravings, book illustrations, business cards, and political cartoons. He even advertised himself as a dentist, specializing in teeth cleaning and wiring in false teeth, which he carved from walrus ivory.

Paul Revere was involved with the Sons of Liberty before the war. At 10 PM on April 18, 1775, he received word from his friend and fellow patriot, Dr. Joseph Warren, and rode to Lexington to warn John Hancock and Sam Adams of the British approach. Apart from his famous "ride," Revere had an undistinguished military career during the war. He died at 83, survived by only 5 of his 16 children. His obituary read, "Seldom has the tomb closed upon a life so honorable and useful."

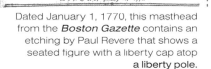

Dated January 1, 1770, this masthead from the **Boston Gazette** contains an etching by Paul Revere that shows a seated figure with a liberty cap atop **a liberty pole.**

A liberty pole

Influenced by the Americans, Arbres de la liberté ("Liberty Trees") became a symbol of the Fench Revolution.

Won't THIS make a great set of dentures!

PAUL REVERE

POOR WALRUS

Gee, I wish he'd stick to silversmithing.

ALEXANDER HAMILTON

In 1790, Secretary of the Treasury Alexander Hamilton formed the U.S. Revenue Cutter Service to enforce customs laws. The ships flew a flag of 15 vertical stripes for the 15 states that were in existence when the service was founded. The idea was to have a flag distinctly different from those being flown by the merchant ships. An act of Congress created the modern day Coast Guard in 1915. The 15 stripes from the original flag remain.

FLAG OF THE U.S. REVENUE CUTTER SERVICE

THE CIVIL FLAG

Revere's fourth son, Joseph Warren Revere (b.1777), was named after his friend, Dr. Joseph Warren who had died in the war 2 years earlier (See letter "P").

In King's Chapel, Boston, one of the bells cast by Revere's foundry still tolls.

The flag, designed by Oliver Wolcott who replaced Alexander Hamilton as Secretary of the Treasury, again used the vertical stripes to denote the civilian authority under the Treasury rather than the military authority under the War Department. **The Civil Flag** was flown during peacetime in custom houses.

What's a custom house?

It's a place near a port where documents are brought to officials by shipping agents in order to pay a duty (tax) on imports or exports.

UNITED STATES COAST GUARD 1790

SEMPER PARTUS
ALWAYS READY
PRESENT COAST GUARD FLAG

is for the USA, united *we'll stand.

Flag of the 2nd New Hampshire Regiment • 1775

*UNITED • Joined, made to agree, cemented, mixed, attached by growth.

† "How good and pleasant it is when brothers live in unity."
Psalm 133:1

 BE CIVIL TO ALL; SOCIABLE TO MANY; FAMILIAR WITH FEW; FRIEND TO ONE; ENEMY TO NONE.

POOR RICHARD'S ALMANACK

47

UNITED
from Middle English "uniten"

CONTINENTAL CURRENCY
Issued in 1776, the Continental was worth 1/3 dollar. The paper, made in Chester County, PA, contained blue fibers and mica flakes.

1

UNIRE, UNIT, UNUS....ONE

YUM!

VIRGIL

We Are One

The device in the center of the 2nd Regiment New Hampshire flag was designed by Benjamin Franklin. The symbol, with 13 interlocking rings, each with a state's name on it and a sunburst with "We Are One" in the center, also appears on Continental currency as well as a minted Continental dollar.

E PLURIBUS UNUM

This drawing comes from Thomas Jefferson's papers

"OUT OF MANY, ONE"

Artist Pierre Eugene du Simitiére chose this Latin expression for his Great Seal design in 1777. (See page S.) The motto was familiar to well-read Americans of the 18th century. It had been seen in London since 1731 on the title page of *The Gentlemen's Magazine's Annual Volumes,* which held a collection of 12 editions of the magazine. The editors of *GM* had taken the phrase *e pluribus unum* from a line in the Roman poet Virgil's poem, "Moretum:" *"color est e pluribus unus"* refers to the making of a salad.

Quotes from Virgil were also used on the other side of the seal. *Annuit Coeptis* is from "Georgics" and *Novus Ordo Seclorum* comes from his "Eclogue."

Pierre Eugene du Simitiére

Born in Geneva, Switzerland, Du Simitiére was skilled in portraiture and heraldry. He designed the state seals for Delaware and Virginia and painted portraits of the famous men of the Revolution. Because his portraits were done from life, they have been accepted by scholars as accurate representations of the subjects. Du Simitiére was also an avid collector of all things American and started the first American museum.

United Colonies of New England
1643

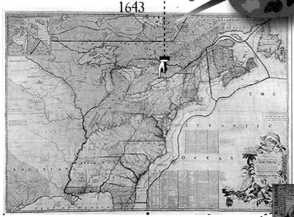

...or the New England Confederation

was a union formed in 1643 by the colonies of Massachusetts Bay, Plymouth, Connecticut, and New Haven for "mutual safety and welfare." Meeting in Boston, representatives from each colony addressed boundary disputes and coordinated defense. The Confederation soon showed signs of weakness. Its commissioners had too little power and Massachusetts Bay, the largest colony of the group, felt that because it was contributing more fighting men and taxes it should have a louder voice. By 1665 they agreed to meet only once every three years. Ten years later things changed. Mounting difficulties with the local Native Americans forced the colonies to unite again to fight what is now called "King Philip's War."

The Continental Congress allowed for the printing of paper dollars or Continental Currency for THE UNITED COLONIES. It reads, "*This bill entitles the Bearer to SEVEN Spanish milled DOLLARS, or the value thereof in Gold or Silver, according to the Resolutions of the Congress held at Philadelphia, the 10th of May 1775.*"

What's a Spanish milled dollar

In use from 1732-1826, the *Spanish milled dollar* was the term given to minted Spanish *reales* by English speakers. The term *milled* means that coin blanks were made on a milling machine and therefore were of uniform size and weight. Because of this process they became the basis of the world's monetary system.

Metacomet was the son of Massasoit, aide to the Pilgrims, when they first landed.

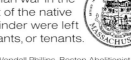
King Philip's War

By 1675, Native Americans were reduced in numbers through death, disease and integration into the colonial culture. Angry, they decided to strike back at New Englanders The Chief of the Pokanokets, **Metacomet,** created a military alliance of 2/3 of those who remained. Called *King Philip* by the English, he led an attack on Swansea, Mass. During the next year, 12 of the 90 towns in New England were destroyed, with hundreds of victims on both sides. In this last major Indian war in the Northeast, 5 percent of the English population died. Forty percent of the native population were either killed or left the region. The remainder were left to serve as slaves, servants, or tenants.

"Crispus Attucks is in the foremost rank of the men that dared." Wendall Phillips, Boston Abolitionist

CRISPUS ATTUCKS

One of those Native Americans who attacked Swansea was a Natick, Prince Yonger. His descendant, Nancy Attucks, was the mother of felled patriot Crispus Attucks. Crispus ran away from his master in Framingham, Massachussetts at the age of 27 and found work as a harpoonist on a whaling ship. In 1770, he was working as a dock hand in Boston, a city which at that time was rife with political tensions, for the British were doing much to provoke the citizenry. On March 5, 1770, while the townspeople were throwing snowballs at the Royal troops, 6' 2" Attucks was among those armed with sticks. The soldiers opened fire and hit Crispus with 2 musket balls. Four others were killed and 6 wounded on that day, which the colonists soon came to describe as **The Boston Massacre**. Attucks' body lay in state as an early martyr for liberty. Until the signing of the *Declaration*, March 5th was celebrated as Crispus Attucks Day.

is for vigilance, which freedom demands.

DON'T TREAD ON ME

VIGILANCE · Watchfulness; attention of the mind in discovering and guarding against danger or providing for safety.

"So then, let us not be like others who are asleep, but let us be alert and self-controlled." 1 Thessalonians 5:6

LITTLE STROKES, FELL GREAT OAKS.

POOR RICHARD'S ALMANACK

"The price of freedom is eternal vigilance."

THOMAS JEFFERSON

Minutemen

In colonial America, men formed armed groups called **militias** to protect their towns from foreign invasion and the effects of war. From these militias small bands of elite fighters were selected by their captains. These soldiers were usually about 25 years of age or younger and were chosen for their enthusiasm, reliability, and physical strength. First to arrive at the battle scene, they were given the title "Minutemen" by the provincial Congress of Massachusetts, which voted in October 1774 to enroll 12,000 men. Concord, Massachusetts, one of the first towns to comply, enrolled 100 Minutemen from their militia roll of 400 members.

Though quick to respond, the Minutemen had their loyalties tied to their home towns and lacked central leadership. This weakness in command led to their demise. After Congress authorized a Continental Army under George Washington, the Minutemen units eventually ceased to exist.

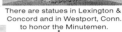

There are statues in Lexington & Concord and in Westport, Conn. to honor the Minutemen.

The Snowshoemen?

Most think the Minutemen formed during the Revolutionary War, but they actually had their roots in the mid-17th century. As early as 1645, men were selected to be dressed and ready within a half hour of being called. In 1689, a unit called "The Snowshoemen," equipped with a "good pair of snowshoes, pair of *moggisons*, a matchlock and a hatchet," prepared to march at a moment's notice to protect the Maine frontier.

THE MATCHLOCK

was the first firearm to have a trigger mechanism for firing. *Matchlock* refers to the type of lock mechanism used for igniting the gun's powder. It was later replaced by the flintlock.

Weaknesses of the **matchlock** caused it to be replaced. The wick constantly needed to be lit for the gun to work. *BUT* damp weather made it hard to stay lit *AND* at night the wick would glow in the dark and give away the soldier's location!

Flintlock

A Minuteman Prepares for War

Early in the Revolutionary War, men were drilled in a half a day training session. Pay vouchers were given to the captains in charge of the program. This is the voucher for Captain Noah Griswold from the 3rd Military Co. in Windsor, Connecticut for the sum of "19 pounds, 8 schillings."

Lobsterbacks

The patriots called the British grenadiers "lobsterbacks" because of their red coats. Lobsters in colonial times weren't considered a delicacy. They were so plentiful along the shoreline that you could pick up more than you could carry. Only the very poor people ate them; others used them for fertilizer.

★ MOST FAMOUS MINUTEMAN ★

Paul Revere

Whooping Crane
Grus americana

Blue is for vigilance

Paul Revere is considered one of the most famous of the Minutemen. His historic ride from Boston to Lexington to alert fellow patriots Samuel Adams and John Hancock was immortalized in the poem by William Wadsworth Longfellow, **"The Midnight Ride of Paul Revere."** By the time the British, in search of stored weapons and supplies, arrived in Lexington, the two had escaped. The Grenadiers were instead met by Captain Jonas Parker and 75 armed Minutemen. They were outnumbered. The British opened fire, killing 8 and injuring 10. Paul Revere was later captured in nearby Concord. Other messengers alerted the local townspeople who, in turn, moved the ammunition and arms to new hiding places, allowing the British to destroy only some of the supplies. The Lobsterbacks headed back to Boston with the Minutemen nipping at their heels the whole way. In the day's fighting the casualty count was high: 73 British dead, 174 wounded; 50 Patriots dead, 39 wounded. The Minuteman Statue now stands where the American position was taken on the side of the Concord River.

In the art of heraldry (the making of coats of arms), colors or tinctures were selected purposefully. The color blue, also known as azure, denoted vigilance, perseverance and justice. Animals were also depicted symbolically. In heraldry, a crane holding a rock was used to show *vigilance*.

Why a crane?

Legend had it that cranes, once living on the banks of the Nile, were being preyed upon by Pygmies, a tribe of diminutive people from equatorial Africa. As protection at night, the flock of cranes would put one bird on watch. The chosen "watchbird" would hold a stone in its claw. If it fell asleep, the dropped stone would awaken the bird. The name of the stone, in French heraldry, is "vigilance".

W is for Washington, who's first in our hearts.

George Washington's personal flag · 1777 · Valley Forge, Pennsylvania

* WASHINGTON • 1ST in war, 1ST in peace, 1ST in the hearts of his countrymen.

"Do you see a man skilled in his work? He will serve before kings; he will not serve before obscure men." *Proverbs 22:29*

WHAT IS MORE VALUABLE THAN GOLD? DIAMONDS. THAN DIAMONDS? VIRTUE.

POOR RICHARD'S ALMANACK

51

*"First in war, first in peace and first in the hearts of his countrymen…
second to none in the humble and endearing scenes of private life."*

Colonel Henry Lee (1756-1818)

George Washington

Washington was born on February 22, 1732, into a planter family in Westmoreland County, Virginia. His father, who died when George was 11, left most of his property to his 2 oldest sons. At age 16, he helped survey land for Thomas Lord Fairfax. Brother Lawrence urged him to join the British Navy, but George's mother refused to agree. When Lawrence died of tuberculosis in 1752, George inherited Mt. Vernon. Two years later he was commissioned as a Lieutenant Colonel in the early days of the French and Indian War. As an aide-de-camp to General Edward Braddock, he escaped injury, though 4 bullets ripped through his coat and 2 horses were shot from under him.

From 1759 to the outbreak of the Revolutionary War, he was at Mt. Vernon managing his land and serving in Virginia's House of Burgesses. He married widowed Martha Custis, the mother of 2 small children. When the 2nd Continental Congress assembled in Philadelphia during May 1775, Washington was appointed Commander in Chief of the Continental Army, a position he held until the end of the war.

After the war, although he wished to retire to Mt. Vernon, George realized that the **Articles of Confederation** were not working well and became a supporter of the Constitutional Convention in 1787. When the new **Constitution** was ratified, George Washington was unanimously elected president, an office he held for 2 terms.

His presidency over, Washington enjoyed his 3-year retirement at Mt. Vernon. On December 12, he was caught in sleet and snow while riding over his farms. An illness developed called "quinsy," a respiratory infection causing a throat inflammation, and he died 2 days later. The young nation mourned the loss of their beloved leader.

EXITUS ACTA PROBAT
"the end proves the deed"
The motto in GW's bookplate

Martha Dandridge Custis Washington

Martha Custis was a 26-year old wealthy widow with two children (John, 4 and Martha, 2) when she met George Washington while he was on leave from the French and Indian War. They were married in her home, ironically called "The White House," on January 6, 1759.

A devoted wife, her life was filled with personal sadness. Two of her 4 children died as toddlers. Her daughter, "Patsy," died at the age of 17 from an epileptic seizure and her son, John died of camp fever at age 22, just as the war had ended. She and George had no children of their own.

When her beloved husband died, Martha closed up their bedroom and moved to a small room on the 3rd floor at Mt. Vernon. Before she died 2 years later, she destroyed their correspondence. Only 2 letters survived, caught behind a drawer in her writing desk.

The U.S. Northern Command shield has 13, 6-pointed stars which it took from GW's personal flag.

George Washington's personal flag dates back to 1775. It went wherever he traveled. Its 6-pointed stars are from English heraldry where they meant "honor, achievement, hope."

The original flag is now at Valley Forge National Historical Park.

Adopted in 1927, the flag of the the 42nd state, Washington, is the only U.S. flag with a president's picture on it.

Scarlet Oak
quercus coccinea

Although there are over 3,700 cherry trees in Washington, DC, the official tree of the District is the Scarlet Oak. The flowering cherry trees (Yoshimo variety), a gift from Japan in 1912, are located around the memorials near the Potomac.

The official bird is the Wood Thrush!

Col. "Light Horse Harry"

Henry Lee was given his nickname for his skill as a horseman during the Revolutionary War. Upon the death of George Washington, Col. Lee was asked by Congress to deliver a tribute to his former commander, from which the words above were excerpted. One of Lee's sons was General Robert E. Lee.

MOUNT VERNON

Originally named "Little Hunting Creek," George Washington expanded the plantation from 2,000 to 8,000 acres; 3,000 were under cultivation.

"No estate in United America is more pleasingly situated." GW

THE WASHINGTON MEMORIAL

To honor our first president, L'Enfant originally had envisioned a grand equestrian statue of GW on the Mall. After his death, a giant square mausoleum was proposed, but Mt. Vernon would not give up his casket. The current obelisk, begun in 1848, was halted during the Civil War and left unfinished until 1876 when it was named a national memorial. Dedicated in 1885, it was opened to the public in 1888.

THOMAS JEFFERSON CALLED DC "THE INDIAN SWAMP."

"FEDERAL" COMES FROM THE LATIN **FOEDUS**

The Latin *foedus* means "Covenant." Thus, in a "Federal" government, a covenant or an agreement has been made between the governed and their elected leaders.

The Federal City

Originally inhabited by Piscataway Tribe, the area where Washington, DC is located was known in Algonquian as **Patawomeke** or "place where people meet." The site was proposed by Alexander Hamilton so that the new nation's capital would not be in any of the states. When President Washington was asked to select the site, not surprisingly, he picked an area near his home. Both Virginia and Maryland ceded 100 sq. miles of land along the Potomac River, establishing "the territory of Columbia" (later called **District**) for "The Federal City - the City of Washington."

Washington selected Pierre Charles L'Enfant to design the city. He laid it out in quadrants with the major avenues leading to the center, where he envisioned placing the Capitol Building. Washington asked Andrew Ellicott and his assistant and friend, Benjamin Banneker, an African-American mathematician, to survey the land.

As early as 1791, people started referring to the new capital as "the city of Washington" but Washington modestly continued to refer to it as "The Federal City." In 1800, the government moved from Philadelphia to its new home. (Pennsylvania Avenue was given a place of prominence by L'Enfant to offset their loss of prestige when the Capitol was moved from Philadelphia.) During the War of 1812, the British burned the Capitol, the president's house and other federal buildings. In 1846, the land originally belonging to Virginia was returned. Now 68 square miles, 40 percent of Washington, D.C. is federally owned.

Letter from Thomas Jefferson to Banneker dated August 30, 1791, in which he expressed his belief that blacks possess talents equal to those "of other colors of men."

The son and grandson of slaves, **Benjamin Banneker** learned to read from his grandmother's *Bible*. A mathematician and astronomer, Banneker wrote his own almanac. Early abolitionists pointed to his accomplishments as proof that the black man should not be enslaved.

is for explorers* who discovered these parts.

The flag of France, the Fleur de Lys, was carried by French explorers

* EXPLORER • One who searches for the purpose of making discovery, to view with care.

"In his heart a man plans his course, but the Lord determines his steps."
Proverbs 16:9

No Gains without Pains

Poor Richard's Almanack

"Discover and investigate...whatsoever islands, countries, regions, or provinces of heathens and infidels, in whatsoever part of the world placed, which before this time were unknown to all Christians."

Patent of Henry VII to John Cabot, 1497

Where is Hy-Brasil?

Giovanni Caboto was an early explorer and the first Italian to reach the mainland of the New World. He was born in 1455 in Gaeta, near Naples. Like his hero, Marco Polo, Cabot wished to find a trade route to Asia. After being refused support by Spain and Portugal, Cabot arrived in England in 1495 with his wife and 3 sons. With a sponsorship from King Henry VII, he set sail on May 20, 1497, looking for **Hy-Brasil,** an island, according to Celtic legend, somewhere in the Atlantic. Instead on June 24, 1497, Cabot, on board his tiny ship the "Matthew" with an 18-member crew, found Canada. When he returned to England, Cabot was rewarded with a pension of 20£ a year and a patent for a new journey. The next year he left, this time with 5 ships. One of the ships stopped in Ireland for needed repairs. The other 4, including one with Cabot aboard, were never heard from again.

"...floating over waves of jasper, far Hy-Brasil in the West."
Hy-Brasil, Henry Kendall (1841-82)

Drawn on maps as early as 1325, **Hy-Brasil** was reported to be west of Ireland. Also called "Fortunate Island," it was said to be shrouded in fog and would appear every 7 years. Those who visited there claimed to have seen golden roofs and domes, fat cattle, and wealthy citizens.

fleur de lys

A stylized flower that many believe is an iris, the symbol of the *fleur de lys* dates back to Mesopotamia. During the Middle Ages when most monarchs were selecting animals on their coats-of-arms, Louis VII (1137-80) adopted the fleur de lys. From that time it was associated with French royalty. It was considered a symbol of the Trinity.

Henry Hudson

In 1608, Henry Hudson was hired to find a **Northeast Passage** to China. They got as far as Norway, when ice floes inhibited their movements. To quell a mutiny, Hudson changed course to look instead for a **Northwest Passage**. They reached the coast of Maine and headed southward, stopping at the North Carolina Outer Banks. The ship then turned to the north and explored the Delaware Bay. Landing at points along the Jersey shore, Hudson then sailed up the river which today bears his name. He went as far as Albany, New York, and claimed the region for the Dutch.

In 1614, 6 years before the Pilgrims landed, the Dutch established a trading post in Fort Nassau. The first settlements in CT, DE, NJ, NY, and PA were all built by the Dutch. It was called *Nieuw Nederlandt* or New Netherland. The Dutch control of the area was short-lived, however, and by the end of the 17th century, all of Nieuw Nederlandt had become a possession of the British Crown. Today, only the names of towns and rivers give evidence to the Dutch presence.

HALF MOON
(in Dutch, Halve Maen)
Commissioned for the Dutch East India Co., it was fitted to support a captain and crew of 20.

Names like: Brooklyn, ▮▮▮▮, Coney Island, Flushing, Hempstead, Hoboken, Nassau, Staten Island, & Yonkers ▮▮▮▮
all have Dutch origins.

Jacques Cartier

Samuel Champlain

Cartier's exploration of northern America for France was continued by Samuel Champlain (1567-1635). The son of a sea captain, Champlain learned sailing from his uncle, who took him on a voyage to the West Indies and New Spain. In 1603 he teamed up with a fur trader and together they explored the "riviére de Canada," the St. Lawrence River. He discovered the lake now named after him and was the first European to set foot in Vermont and New York (1609). He also explored the coastline of Maine, then called Acadia. In 1633, Champlain was named governor of Quebec, the capital of New France. As governor, he founded a college where children of the native tribes were taught French. He died of a stroke there two years later.

Jacques Cartier was born on St. Malo, an island off the coast of France. Hoping to find a water route to Asia, Francis I commissioned him to search for the Northwest Passage. In 1534, not finding China, Cartier instead explored Canada and what is now New England and claimed the land for France. On a second voyage he sailed up the river St. Laurent, built a fort named Quebec, and established the town of Mont Real (Mount Royal), now Montreal.

Cartier and his men wintered in Canada in a Huron village. Twenty-five of his men died of scurvy. Later, betraying the generosity of his hosts, Cartier kidnapped 12 Hurons including their chief. He was hoping the prisoners would tell him where their gold mine was located but there was no mine. He died in 1557 in France without much recognition.

Oops!

Verrazano made contact with the native peoples at each of his stops. His third and last voyage took him to the West Indies, where the natives were less friendly. **They were cannibals** and had him for lunch!

On Acadia, Champlain saw mountainous areas that were bare and rocky. He called it *Isles des Monts Desert.* It is now known as Mt. Desert Island.

I ♥ NY

Giovanni da Verrazano

Sponsored by Francis I, Verrazano set out in 1525 with his mapmaker brother, Girolamo, and crew to explore and map out the New World. Together they traveled up the Eastern coast of America from the Outer Banks in North Carolina, past New York Harbor, Newport, Rhode Island, and the coast of Maine. At New Foundland he headed back to France. He made two other voyages.

Verrazano-Narrows Bridge

In 1923, a "Liberty Bridge" was proposed to span the NYC boroughs of Staten Island and Brooklyn. Work began in 1959 on the world's longest suspension bridge, 4,260 ft. in length. Completed in 1964, it was named after Giovanni da Verrazano, the first European to reach New York Harbor (1524).

DON'T try walking over the VNB ...there's no pedestrian walkway!

Oops! Scurvy!

Scurvy, a vitamin C deficiency, was a common ailment among seamen. In 1540, Jacques Cartier had learned of a remedy for the disease from Native Americans in Canada....pine needles in hot water. Yum. Although first described by the Dutch physician Echthius in 1541, it wasn't until 100 years had passed that Dr. James Lind convinced the British navy to include limes, not pine needles, in the diet for seamen. The sailors were then nick-named "limeys."

SCURVY LEADS TO:
· LOOSE TEETH
· BLEEDING GUMS
· ANEMIA
· SLOW WOUND HEALING

is for yearning hearts crossing the sea.

The flag of Maryland containing the arms-banner of Lord Baltimore.

YEARNING · To feel an earnest desire; to have a strong inclination stretching toward a desired object or end.

 "Hope deferred makes the heart sick, but a longing fulfilled is a tree of life."

Proverbs 13:12

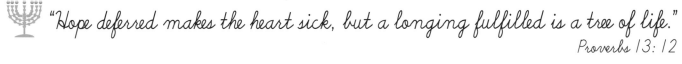 THE HEART OF A FOOL IS IN HIS MOUTH, BUT THE MOUTH OF A WISE MAN IS IN HIS HEART.

POOR RICHARD'S ALMANACK

"Give me your tired, your poor, your huddled masses yearning to breathe free..."

Emma Lazarus
(1849 - 87)

Emma Lazarus grew up in a prominent, wealthy, fourth-generation Jewish-American family in New York City. She was well-educated and by the age of 25 was a published author and poet. In 1883, she wrote "New Colossus" for a fund-raising auction to help construction costs of the Statue of Liberty's pedestal. By 1886, the statue was erected in New York Harbor. Emma died the next year while visiting in France. She never saw the impact of her work, for it wasn't until 1901 that her poem was added on a bronze plaque at the base of the statue.

What's my real name?

a) Mother of Exiles
b) Liberty Enlightening the World
c) Lady Liberty

the answer is "b".

"Keep, ancient lands, your storied pomp!" cries she with silent lips.
"Give me your tired, your poor,
Your huddled masses yearning to breathe free,
The wretched refuse of your teeming shore.
Send these, the homeless, tempest-tossed to me,
I lift my lamp beside the golden door!"

Emma Lazarus
November 2, 1883

NOT ACTUAL SIZE

The 7 spikes in the crown symbolize the 7 seas of the modern world: • **Arctic**
Antarctic
North and South Atlantic
North and South Pacific
and the Indian Ocean

There are 25 windows in the crown representing the 25 gemstones found on earth.

Her sandal is 25 feet long. She'd wear a women's shoe size of 879!

Located on 12 acres in New York Harbor, the Statue of Liberty was a gift of friendship from the people of France. Revered by Americans, the statue is also considered a universal symbol of freedom and democracy.

Sculptor Frederic-Auguste Bartholdi was commissioned to create a statue which commemorated the centennial of the American Revolution. Because of the structural problems that he knew would arise while designing a huge copper sculpture, Bartholdi enlisted the aid of Alexandre Gustave Eiffel, of Eiffel Tower fame. Eiffel was asked to design a secondary framework which would allow the statue's copper skin to move independently, yet is supported to stand upright.

The Americans were responsible to pay for the pedestal on which the statue would stand. With the help of philanthropist Joseph Pulitzer, funds were obtained to complete it. The statue was constructed in France. To allow for a safe journey across the Atlantic, it was reduced to 350 pieces packed in 214 crates. It took 4 months to reassemble. President Grover Cleveland dedicated the statue on October 28, 1886. It was designated a national monument on October 15, 1924.

Fun Statue Facts

- Used 179,200 lbs. of copper

- total weight: 450,000 lbs.

- 354 steps to reach the crown, 192 to reach the pedestal

- size of fingernail: 13" X 10"

- length of hand: 16' 5"

- length of nose: 4' 6"

- the tablet held in her left hand says: "July IV, MDCCLXXVI," Roman numerals for the day of America's independence from Britain, July 4, 1776

Bartholdi's design patent, granted February 18, 1879.

Frederic Auguste Bartholdi

Alexandre Gustave Eiffel

Ellis Island was originally called **Kioshk** or Gull Island by local Native Americans.

Ellis Island

I ♥ Ellis Island
...we called it Gibbet Island

gibbet

another word for *gallows*

Samuel Ellis gained ownership of the island in the late 1700s. Prior to becoming an entry spot for immigrants, Ellis Island had been a hanging place for pirates, a harbor fort, and a munitions & ordinance depot called Fort Gibson. Originally barely 3 acres, Ellis Island grew to its present 27 acres with the help of ship ballast and landfill from digging NYC's subway system.

Prior to 1890, individual states controlled immigration. But the large masses of immigrants at the end of the 19th century proved too much for the old system. The federal government bought Ellis Island and set up a processing station there. The peak period of mass immigration was from 1880 -1924. When quota laws were enacted, the numbers dropped sharply. By 1924, Ellis Island had become a detention center. During WW II approximately 7,000 German, Italian and Japanese aliens and citizens were detained there. In 1954, no longer needed, the facility was closed.

Ten years later, President Lyndon B. Johnson declared the island part of the Statue of Liberty National Monument. It now houses a renovated complex which is visited by almost 2 million visitors annually.

One of the oldest symbols of the Jewish faith and once used in the ancient temple, the 7- branched menorah has become a symbol of the State of Israel and its mission to be *"a light unto the nations"* (Isa. 42:6).

Political instability ·
Poor economic conditions ·
Religious intolerence ·

...in Europe were the top reasons for the mass influx of immigrants to America from 1880-1924.

is for Zealous* heroes who love liberty.

Flown by John Paul Jones on his ship, *Serapis,* in the Revolutionary War

ZEALOUS · Warmly engaged or ardent in the pursuit of an object; passionate.

⚓ *"Diligent hands will rule, but laziness ends in slave labor."*
Proverbs 12:24

 HIDE NOT YOUR TALENTS, THEY FOR USE WERE MADE; WHAT'S A SUN-DIAL IN THE SHADE?

POOR RICHARD'S ALMANACK

57

"I am not a Virginian, but an American."

Patrick Henry · October 14, 1774
Speech to The First Continental Congress

Called the "African Hero" by Richard Henry Lee, Lord Dunmore offered to free any African or Native American **IF** he would join the British army. Black mothers started calling their newborns "Dunmore" in his honor.

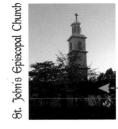

John Murray, Lord Dunmore

Born in Hanover County, Virginia, in 1736, Patrick Henry received his education at home. After studying on his own, Henry took his law exam in Williamsburg in 1760. Elected to the Virginia House of Burgesses, he argued for resolutions against the Stamp Act of 1765. An outspoken leader against British tyranny, Henry's speeches were "torrents of sublime eloquence," according to Thomas Jefferson. Besides serving in the House of Burgesses, Henry was a delegate to the Virginia Constitution Ratification Convention and became the first governor of Virginia under its new constitution, serving 3 terms. President George Washington appointed him to be Secretary of State in 1795, but Henry declined. Later, President John Adams asked him to be an envoy to France, but failing health caused him to decline that position as well. Patrick Henry died in 1799 at the age of 63 in his family home, Red Hill.

St. John's Episcopal Church

In March 1775, 120 Virginia leaders including George Washington, Thomas Jefferson, Richard Henry Lee, his brother Francis Lightfoot Lee, Patrick Henry, and others met in this Richmond church to avoid angering the Royal Governor, Lord Dunmore, in Williamsburg. It was here that Henry gave his famous "Liberty or Death" speech.

"...one of the garden spots of Virginia"
Patrick Henry describing Red Hill

RED HILL

The **Osage Orange** tree became popular in the East after Lewis and Clark's 1804 expedition. Its wood was used by the Osage Tribe in Missouri to make bows. An example of the species is located on the grounds of Red Hill. Reaching 55 ft. and spanning 90 ft. wide, the 330-year-old tree is the oldest and largest of its kind in America.

Osage Orange
maclura pomifera

Samuel Adams
..."the greatest incendiary in the empire."
**Thomas Hutchinson
Royal Governor of Massachusetts**

"It does not require a majority to prevail, but rather an irate, tireless minority keen to set brush fires in people's minds."

A graduate of Harvard who failed in the mercantile business, Samuel Adams entered politics full-time and was elected to the Massachusetts legislature. He became a vocal critic when the British government passed tax laws, especially the **Tea Act**. He urged a boycott of British goods after the **Intolerable Acts** were passed. In 1774, the Massachusetts Legislature sent Adams to the First Continental Congress and then later to the Second Continental Congress. He was a signer of the **Declaration of Independence,** as was his cousin, John Adams. After the war ended, Adams was elected Massachusetts' lieutenant governor, an office he held until 1794 when the governor, John Hancock, died. Adams was then elected governor and retired from that post in 1797. He died October 2, 1803, at the age of 82.

Thomas Hutchinson

This is the only portrait of Hutchinson that has survived. He was so fiercely hated that any likeness would have been destroyed by his enemies.

A descendant of Anne Hutchinson, a founder of Rhode Island, Thomas Hutchinson entered Harvard at the age of 12, graduating 4 years later. When the colonies began to speak of independence, he became a Loyalist. As governor of Massachusetts, many Bostonians blamed him for the **Stamp Act**. His residence sacked, he barely escaped with his life. After the Boston Massacre he wrote to his superiors, "Boston is pitched into perfect frenzy." Replaced by a military governor, General Thomas Gage, Hutchinson sailed to London, where he died in 1780.

TODAY'S VERSION OF
BONHOMME RICHARD

What's a Serapis?

SERAPIS

Created by Ptolemy I (323 BC - 285 BC), this Greco-Egyptian deity combined Osiris and Apis to serve as a provider of healing and medicine. Greeks portrayed him with long hair and a long beard.

Serapis Flag

JOHN PAUL JONES

"I wish to have no connection with any ship that does not sail fast, for I intend to go in harm's way."

Born in Scotland, the fourth son of an estate gardener, John Paul went to sea as a third mate on a slaver at age 17. Calling it an "abominable trade," Paul quit. By his 21st birthday he had, by his own merits, become captain of his own ship. As a merchant ship captain, he killed a mutinous sailor in the West Indies in self-defense. Fleeing to the United States, Paul arrived in Virginia in 1773 as John Jones. Later he changed his name to **John Paul Jones** to avoid reprisals. When Congress created the Continental Navy, Jones, although not an American citizen, offered his services and in 1775 was commissioned as a 1st Lieutenant on the **Alfred**. Quickly rising to the rank of captain, Jones conducted sea raids on the coast of Britain, creating such havoc that the British Admiralty issued orders to hang him as a pirate if captured. In 1779, he took command of the **USS Bonhomme Richard**, named in honor of Ben Franklin's Poor Richard. Later that year he engaged the British frigate, **Serapis**, in the North Sea. It was during this battle that Jones uttered his now famous "Sir, I have not yet begun to fight." The American crew boarded the **Serapis** after the British had **struck her colors** and from her deck watched as their own ship sank into the sea. After the war, he remained in Europe, dying of pneumonia in Paris at age 45. He was buried in an unmarked grave in a Protestant cemetery. In 1845, Col. J.H. Shelburne began a campaign to return Jones' remains to America. After a 6-year systematic search, his remains were found and returned home with an honor convoy of 4 cruisers. He was re-interred at the Naval Academy in Annapolis, Maryland, on January 26, 1913.

"striking her colors"
under international law
...the universal
sign of
surrender

Anchor Cross
Etched in the Catacombs, this early Christian symbol was a covert sign of faith and hope used during the times of Roman persecution.

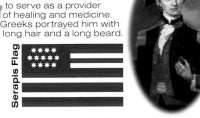

SERAPIS & THE BONHOMME RICHARD

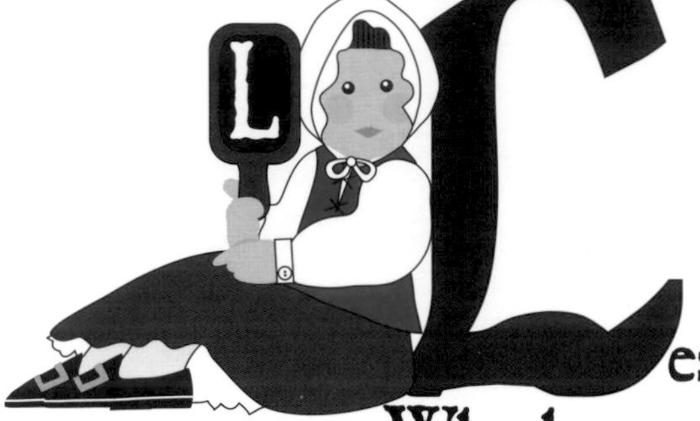

Lessons on Liberty are needed by all,
Whether you're big or whether you're small.
So learn these true lessons and do learn them well,
Then all generations in freedom* will dwell.

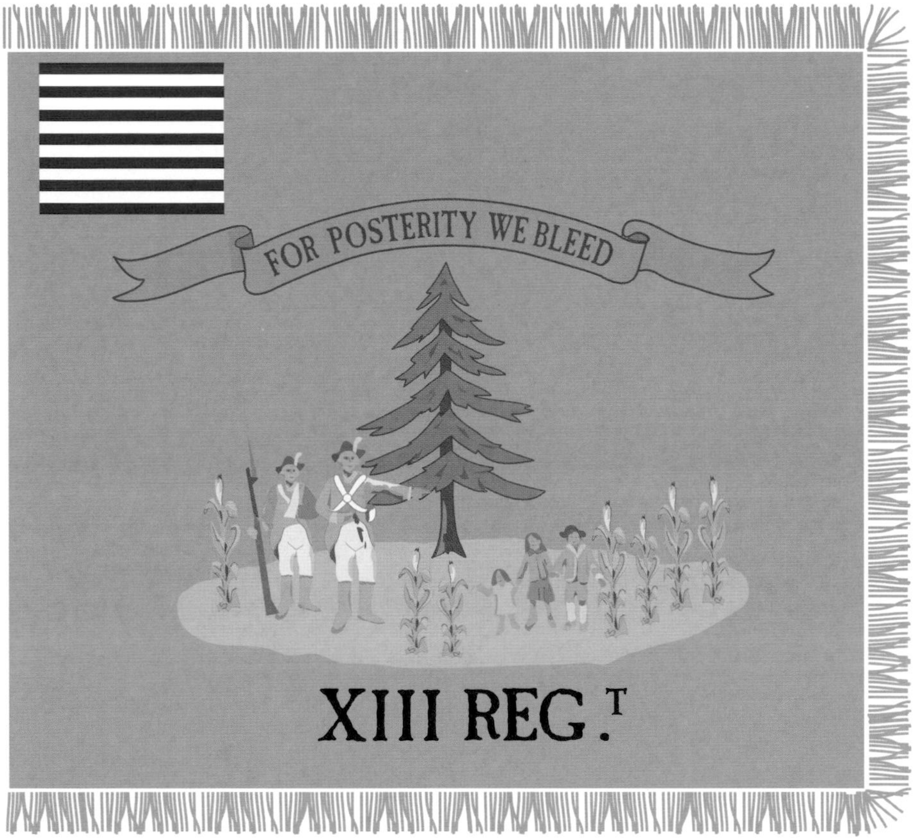
FOR POSTERITY WE BLEED
XIII REG.T

The Standard of the 13th Continental Regiment used in 1776

* **FREEDOM** • A state of exemption from the power or control of another: liberty; exemption from slavery, servitude or confinement. Freedom is personal, civil, political, and religious.

"Train a child in the way he should go, and when he is old he will not turn from it." Proverbs 22:6

WISE MEN LEARN BY OTHERS' HARMS; FOOLS BY THEIR OWN.

POOR RICHARD'S ALMANACK

"Our duty to ourselves, to posterity, and to mankind, call on us by every motive which is sacred or honorable, to watch over the safety of our beloved country ..."

THOMAS JEFFERSON

Posterity

future generations, all of a person's descendants

Middle English "posterite"

ORIGINALLY LATIN "**POSTERUS**"
MEANING..."COMING AFTER"

"By what means this great and important alteration in the religious, moral, political, and social character of the people of thirteen colonies, all distinct, unconnected, and independent of each other, was begun, pursued, and accomplished, it is surely interesting to humanity to investigate, and perpetuate to *posterity*."
A letter to H. Niles by John Adams, February 13, 1818

"*Posterity:* you will never know how much it has cost my generation to preserve your freedom. I hope you will make good use of it."
John Quincy Adams

"To be faithful to ourselves, we must keep our ancestors and *posterity* within reach and grasp of our thoughts and affections, living in the memory and retrospect of the past, and hoping with affection and care for those who are to come after us."
Daniel Webster

"The Constitution of the United States was made not merely for the generation that then existed, but for *posterity*- unlimited, undefined, endless, perpetual *posterity.*"
Henry Clay, US Senator

"It is not merely for today, but for all time to come that we should perpetuate for *our children's children* this great and free government, which we have enjoyed all our lives."
Abraham Lincoln
to the 166th Ohio Regiment,
August 22, 1864

the canterbury cross

Celtic in origin, the Canterbury Cross dates from 850 AD. It was excavated beneath St. George Street, Canterbury, England, in 1867 and is presently on display in a museum in Canterbury Cathedral.

For the uniform of the 13th Regiment you needed per coat:

1 3/4 yards blue broadcloth

1 1/4 yards white or buff

3 large buttons each

6 small buttons each

Finials are decorative ornaments found at the top end of a staff. Spear-pointed or spade-shaped, finials were often used with standards.

FINIAL

The Standard of the 13th Regiment

The original flag has not survived, but has been reconstructed from a description by a 19th century historian. The standard was probably made from silk. The elements on the flag include a small *Sons of Liberty* flag in the upper corner. The pine tree and field of Indian corn are both symbolic of New England. The 2 officers, one of whom is wounded in the chest, are pointing to the 3 children under the tree, who represent the generations to come. Their motto is emblazoned on the top...
FOR POSTERITY WE BLEED.

FOR POSTERITY WE BLEED

XIII REG.ᵀ

STANDARD

The organizational flag of a mounted military unit is the **Standard;** the flag of a dismounted unit is called the *Colors.* It was the most visible symbol of the regiment.

The elder **Edward Wigglesworth,** the Colonel's uncle, taught Ben Franklin at the South Grammar School in Boston when Ben was 8 years old.

Who was Edward Wigglesworth?

Colonel Edward Wigglesworth was born into a prominent Massachusetts family on January 3, 1742. His grandfather, Michael Wigglesworth, had been a minister and a physician. When he died, Cotton Mather, the well-known Puritan preacher, gave his eulogy. Graduating from Harvard in 1761, Edward became a merchant in Newbury, Massachusetts. Wigglesworth joined the army in 1775. A year later, he received his commission as a colonel and began to lead the 13th Continental Regiment of Massachusetts. He left the service in 1779, went home, and then became the captain of a privateering vessel, capturing the crew and cargo of enemy ships. He died on December 8, 1826.

STAFF

XIII REG.ᵀ

The 13th Continental Regiment of Massachusetts was organized on September 8, 1776. Led by **Colonel Edward Wigglesworth,** the group was on duty throughout the war: in the Siege of Boston, Lake Champlain, the Battle of Saratoga, the defense of Philadelphia, the Valley Forge encampment, Rhode Island, and Stony Point, New York. The regiment was disbanded at West Point on January 1, 1781.

LESSONS ON LIBERTY
A PRIMER FOR YOUNG PATRIOTS

THE FAITH OF OUR
FOUNDING FATHER,
GEORGE WASHINGTON

*"I shall always strive to prove a faithful
and impartial patron of genuine, vital religion."*

George Washington, May 29, 1789

While we are zealously performing the duties of good citizens and soldiers we certainly ought not to be inattentive to the higher duties of religion. To the distinguished character of patriot, it should be our highest glory to add the more distinguished character of *Christian*.

General George Washington
General Orders, Headquarters, Valley Forge, May 2, 1778

You do well to wish to learn our arts and ways of life, and above all, the religion of *Jesus Christ.*

General George Washington
Speech to the Delaware Chiefs, Headquarters, Middle Brook Camp, New Jersey, June 2, 1779

I now make it my earnest prayer, that God would have you, and the State over which you preside, in his holy protection, that he would incline the hearts of the citizens to cultivate a spirit of subordination and obedience to government, to entertain a brotherly affection and love for one another, for their fellow citizens of the United States at large, and particularly for their brethren who have served in the field, and finally, that he would most graciously be pleased to dispose us all to do justice, to love mercy, and to demean ourselves with that charity, humility, and pacific temper of mind, which were the characteristics of *the Divine Author of our blessed Religion*, and without an humble imitation of whose example in these things, we can never hope to be a happy nation.

General George Washington
Circulars to the Governors of all 13 States, Headquarters, Newburgh, New York, June 8, 1783

May the same wonder-working Deity, who long since delivering the Hebrews from the Egyptian oppressors planted them in the promised land- whose providential agency has lately been conspicuous in establishing these United States as an independent nation - still continue to water them with the dews of Heaven and to make the inhabitants of every denomination participate in the temporal and spiritual blessings of that people whose *God is Jehovah.*

President George Washington
Letter to the Hebrew Congregation of Savannah, Georgia, May 1790

Of all the dispositions and habits which lead to political prosperity, *Religion and morality are indispensable supports.* In vain would that man claim the tribute of patriotism, who should labor to subvert these great pillars of human happiness, these firmest props of the duties of men and citizens. The mere politician, equally with the pious man, ought to respect and to cherish them. A volume could not trace all their connections with private and public felicity. Let it simply be asked where is the security for property, for reputation, for life, if the sense of religious obligation *desert* the oaths, which are the instruments of investigation in Courts of Justice? And let us with caution indulge the supposi tion, that morality can be maintained without religion. Whatever may be conceded to the influence of refined education on minds of peculiar structure, reason and experience both forbid us to expect that national morality can prevail in exclusion of religious principle.

President George Washington
Farewell Address, Philadelphia, September 17, 1796

JUDEO-CHRISTIAN SYMBOLS
AND THEIR MEANINGS

This cross is named after St. Andrew in the New Testament, one of the Twelve Apostles, brother of Peter. According to tradition he was martyred on an X-shaped cross (**St. Andrew's cross**). This cross is used on the flag of Scotland, where he is their patron saint.

The **Cross Patée** dates back to the Crusades and was used as a sign of divine protection.

The **Jerusalem Cross** dates back to the Crusades. The 4 inner crosses symbolize the Gospel being spread to the 4 corners of the earth.

The **Tau Cross**, made from the Greek letter "T," is the simplest of all crosses. It is often used as the cross of prophecy, or Old Testament cross, because it is the traditional sign that Israelites made with lamb's blood on their doorposts in Egypt on the night of Passover. A tau cross is often pictured as the pole on which Moses lifted up the brazen serpent in the wilderness.

This form of the cross is used primarily in the Russian Orthodox Church. The upper bar represents the inscription, abbreviated "INRI," that Pilate had placed above Jesus' head. The meaning of the slanted bar is lost in legend. One story holds that Jesus' legs were of unequal length, another that the earthquake that came at His death caused the cross to tilt. Another explanation (probably the correct one) is that the slanted bar forms St. Andrew's cross. St. Andrew is believed to have introduced Christianity to Russia.

The **Cross Pommé** has knobs, resembling apples (Pomme is French for apple), which represent the fruits of the Christian life. Since knobs were used on pastoral staffs in ancient times as a symbol of authority, this is sometimes called the Bishop's Cross.

The **Byzantine Cross** is generally used by the Greek Orthodox Church.

This Greek cross is superimposed on a Greek "chi," ✕ , the first letter of the Greek word for "Christ." It forms a cross with 8 arms. Since the number 8 is symbolic of rebirth or regeneration, this cross is often referred to as a baptismal cross.

The **Chi Cross** is from the word ΧΡΙΣΤΟΣ, transliterated as **Christos**, which is Greek for "Christ." Greek is the language in which the New Testament was written.

The **Celtic Cross** evolved in the British Isles, and the earliest forms date from the seventh to ninth centuries in Ireland, Wales, and Scotland. The circle within the Celtic cross is a symbol of eternity and of God's endless love.

Of the several sacred monograms of Christ, the **Chi Rho** is one of the most ancient. It is formed of the Greek letters chi (X) and rho (P). Legend dates it back to the time of Emperor Constantine (274?-337) whose soldiers carried it on their shields as they marched into battle. Grateful for the victory, Constantine issued the **Edict of Milan** in 313 whereby Christians were no longer officially persecuted.

The **Cross Triumphant** symbolizes the final triumph and reign of Christ over the world. It is often used in Christian art atop the scepter of Jesus as He reigns in glory. The circle is an **orb**, a symbol of royalty.

The **Magen David** or Shield of David is more commonly called the "Star of David." Tradition claims it represents the shield of the ancient king of Israel, David, or an image that was on his shield. The symbol gained popularity as a symbol of Judaism during the Zionist movement in 1897, and is now on the flag of the State of Israel.

The **Cross Embattled**, also called the Cross Bretessée, was used in heraldic art. It has ragged outlines like those seen on the battlements of a castle.

The Ionic Cross is the form of the cross taken by Irish-born monk St. Columba (521-597) to the island of Iona, off the coast of Scotland, where he and 12 disciples founded a new monastery.

The **Maltese Cross** dates back to the Crusades as well. It was the symbol of the Knights of St. John who lived for a time on the island of Malta. Legend has it that some of the Knights were attacked and burned by Saracens using naphtha, a volatile liquid occurring naturally (also called crude petroleum). Their comrades-in-arms heroically attempted to rescue them, thus becoming an archetype of our modern-day firefighters who have adopted this as their symbol.

In heraldry, a **Cross Potent** is a cross whose arms end in a short line traveling across at right angles.

St. Peter's Cross is named after Peter who is believed to have been crucified upside down at his own request, for he did not feel worthy to die the same way as Jesus. Many Christians view this cross as a symbol of humility.

With its three buds, this is called the **Budded Cross**. The 3-leafed clover end caps remind believers of the Trinity. It is often used in heraldry.

Called the **Cross Crosslet,** this is a cross formed of 4 smaller crosses. This form represents the spreading of the gospel to the 4 corners of the earth. This ornamental version rests on a lattice forming 4 additional crosses. It is often confused with the **Jerusalem Cross**.

This is called the **Avellane Cross**. A medieval cross, its name is of French origin meaning "nut." The cross ends in filbert husks.

The pointed ends of this Latin cross, or the **Passion Cross**, represent the suffering of Christ at his crucifixion.

The **Four Ermine Spots** pattern, used in heraldic art, mimics the spots on an ermine, a short-tailed weasel. A spotted cross was used in the flag of Nantes, a town in France.

A **Bezant Cross** is composed of bezants joined together. A bezant is a gold roundlet, which represents a coin. It is supposed to have been introduced into English heraldry by the Crusaders, who had received the gold coin while in the East.

Soon after the Edict of Nantes was revoked, the **Huguenot Cross** was worn as a confirmation of faith. The Huguenot Cross is designed in the form of a Maltese cross (4 triangles, each with 2 points, which meet in the center). These points symbolize the eight Beatitudes (Matthew 5: 3-10). Suspended from the lower triangle by a ring of gold is a dove in downward flight, signifying the Holy Spirit. In times of persecution a pearl, symbolizing a teardrop, replaced the dove.

One of the oldest symbols of the Jewish faith once used in the ancient temple, the 7-branched **menorah** has become a symbol of the nation of Israel and its mission to be "a light unto the nations" (Isaiah 42:6).

The **Anchor Cross** symbolizes the Christian's hope in Christ. This cross was also the emblem of St. Clement, Bishop of Rome, who according to tradition was tied to an anchor and tossed into the sea by the emperor Trajan.

The Canterbury Cross is a 9th century Byzantine cross discovered in 1867 on St. George's Street, Canterbury, England. The Canterbury cross dates to circa 850 A.D. and was originally cast in bronze. Its triangular panels etched with a "triquetra" pattern symbolize the Trinity.

Photo & Picture Credits

First Page:

"Ben Franklin." No Date. Online image. Retrieved July 20, 2005. http://www.teachpol.tcnj.edu/amer_pol_hist/fi/0000000f.htm - Ben Franklin

"Open primer." No Date. Online image. Northeastern Illinois University. Retrieved July 20, 2005. http://www.neiu.edu/~ghsingle/nep.jpg - open primer

"Primer cover." No Date. Online image. http://www.wallbuilders.com/store/product17.html Used with permission

"Ram." No Date. Online image. Jernigan's Taxidermy. Retrieved July 20, 2005. http://www.bumsteer.com/ byron/DALL SHEEP.jpg – ram head

"Dame School" No Date. Online image. http://en.wikipedia.org/wiki/Image:Dame_School_1.jpeg PD-art

"George Washington." No Date. Online image. Gilbert Stuart. Retrieved July 20, 2005. http://www.constitution.org/img/george_washington_stuart.jpg - Sitting George.

"Ten Commandments". National Archive plaque. No Date. Online image. American Vision. Retrieved July 20, 2005. http://www.americanvision.org/images/Commandments_in_Gates.jpg - bronze commandments, Carrie Devorah

"Moses". Niehaus, Charles. 1897. Online image. Ethics and Public Policy Center. Retrieved July 20, 2005. http://www.eppc.org/imgLib/20050204_statue1.jpg - Moses statue, Carrie Devorah

"Moses". 1935. Online image. http://www.journeywithjesus.net. Retrieved July 20, 2005. http://www.journeywithjesus.net/Essays/Moses_At_The_US_Supreme_Court_sm.jpg - Moses, ©Carrie Devorah

"Supreme Court Building." No date. Online image. Retrieved July 20, 2005. http://web.utk.edu/~scheb/SCfront.jpg. Photo taken by Professor John M. Scheb, University of Tennessee. Used by his permission.

Letter A:

"Sea Monster" No date. On line image. The 1539 Carta Marina by Olaus Magnus: James Ford Bell Library, University of Minnesota, http://bell.lib.umn.edu/map/OLAUS/lgolaus/maplg.jpg. PD

"Sea Chests." No date. Online image. J.P. Uranker Woodcarver. Retrieved August 18, 2004. http://www.jpuwoodcarver.com/assets/html/sea_chests.htm - sea chest

"Seabiscuit." No date. Online image. Seabiscuit. Retrieved October, 2006. http://pdphoto.org/PictureDetail.php?mat=pdef&pg=8231, PD

"Amerigo Vespucci" No date. Online image. http://en.wikipedia.org/wiki/Image:Amerigo_Vespucci01.jpg - statue of Vespucci, PD-art

"Waldmueller map" No date. Online image.http://en.wikipedia.org/wiki/Image:Ct000725C-wh012_5-Universalis_cosmographia_secundum_Ptholomaei_traditionem_et_Americi_Vespucii_aliorum-que_lustrationes.gif. PD-art

"Columbus' signature". No date. Online image. http://es.wikipedia.org/wiki/Imagen:Firma-colon.JPG - PD

Letter B:

"Cod" No Date. Online image. http://www.photolib.noaa.gov/historic/nmfs/images/big/figb0314.jpg PD-USgov

"Native American" The Story of America. Pleasantville, New York: The Reader's Digest Association, Inc., 1975.

"Moose" No Date. Online image. image.http://images.fws.gov/default.cfm?fuseaction=records.display&CFID=5505842&CFTOKEN=76459007&id=0ED12468%2D1FCB%2D4C31%2D94F35A9D61AA5626 created by Ronald L. Bell, PD-USgov (moose with water drip)

"Oppossum" Thanks to the Delaware Natural History Museum

"Turkeys" Special thanks to David, Delaware Nature Society and Dr. Jean Woods, Curator of Birds, Delaware Natural History Museum"

"Mikey" Photo used with permission. Maryellen McMorrow

"William Bradford Signature." No date. Online Image. MayflowerHistory. com, edited by Caleb Johnson - Bradford signature

Webber, David J. "William Bradford bust." No Date. Online image. Retrieved July 2, 2004. http://www.angelfire.com/ny4/djw/williambradford.html "Pilgrim Society: Pilgriim Hall Museum" - bust

"The Landing of the Pilgrims." No date. Online image. http://homepages.roots.com/julieann/Mayflower_Stephen_Hopkins.htm PD - "The Landing of the Pilgrims."

Letter C:

"Benjamin Franklin" No date. Online Image. http://teachpol.tcnj.edu/amer_pol_hist/fi/0000000f.htm. PD-art– Benjamin Franklin

"James Madison" No date. Online Image. http://en.wikipedia.org/wiki/Image:Jm4.gif. PD-art – Madison

"Turkey" Thanks to Dr. Jean Woods, Curator of Birds, Delaware Natural History Museum

Bailey, Thomas A. and Kennedy, David M. The American Pageant. Lexington, Massachusetts: D.C. Heath and Company, 1987. PD– Constitution cartoon

Letter D:

"Jefferson writing desk" Used with permission. The Smithsonian Museum, National Museum of American History

"Jefferson" No date. Online Image. http://www.answers.com/topic/thomasjefferson-jpg PD

"Declaration of Independence" No date. Online Image. http://en.wikipedia.org/wiki/Image:Us_declaration_independence.jpg PD

"Signature" No date. Online Image. http://en.wikipedia.org/wiki/Image:JohnHancockSignature.jpg PD

"John Hancock" No date. Online Image. http://en.wikipedia.org/wiki/Image:JohnHancockLarge.jpeg PD

"First draft" No date. Online Image. http://www.loc.gov/exhibits/treasures/images/decp1.jpg PD

Letter E:

"Eagle" Used with permission, Professor David Stewart, Hillsdale College

"Eagle in Flight" http://images.fws.gov/default.cfm?fuseaction=records.display&CFID=5505842&CFTOKEN=76459007&id=AFC8BA66%2D764B%2D44D2%2DA814C2BF9268AAEF US Fish and Wildlife Service, PD

"Turkeys" Special thanks to David, Delaware Nature Society and Dr. Jean Woods, Curator of Birds, Delaware Natural History Museum

"Sloop of War Erie". No Date. Online Image. U.S. Brig Niagara. Retrieved September 9, 2005 www.brigniagara.org/shipsofinterest.htm Erie Maritime Museum - General Schuyler sloop

"Burgoyne's Surrender". October 17, 1777. Online Image. http://en.wikipedia.org/wiki/Image:Saratoga_surrender.jpg General Schuyler- Collection of the New York Historical Society

"General Schuyler". Trumbull, John.1792. Online image. Alexander Hamilton. Retrieved July 7, 2004. http://www.alexanderhamiltonexhibition.org/gallery/schuyler_p.html PD - General Schuyler

"Seal." No date. Online image. http://www.photolib.noaa.gov/historic/c&gs/images/big/theb1449.jpg noaa. PD-USgov

Letter F:

"Francis Scott Key." No date. Online image. http://en.wikipedia.org/wiki/Image:Key-Francis-Scott-LOC.jpg PD - Francis Scott Key picture

"Anacreon" No date. Online image. http://en.wikipedia.org/wiki/Image:Anacreon_-_Project_Gutenberg_eText_12788.png PD

"The Battle of Baltimore" George Gray, 1946. Courtesy of the National Park Service, Fort McHenry National Monument and Historic Shrine

"Herbert Hoover" No date. Online Image. http://en.wikipedia.org/wiki/Image:Hhover.gif PD

"Mary Pickersgill." No date. Online Image.http://www.senate.gov/~craig/kidsclub/trav_ssb.htmMary Pickersgill picture PD

"Fort McHenry." "Civil War Prints and Historical Art." Retrieved July 23, 2004. http://www.oldgloryprints.com/mnhenry.htm Image courtesy of Gallon Historical Art, Gettysburg, PA www.gallon.com - Fort McHenry picture

"Fort McHenry." No date. Online image. The Howard County Public School System. Retrieved July 23, 2004. http://www.howard.k12.md.us/res/rm/ftmch/fm3.html - McHenry Flag picture

"Star Spangled Banner." No date. Online image. http://www.bcpl.net/~etowner/fortflag.jpg

"Original Flag" composite photograph of the Star-Spangled Banner, the flag that inspired the national anthem. Smithsonian's National Museum of American History, ©2004

Photo & Picture Credits

Letter G:

"Salmon P. Chase." No date. Online Image. http://lcweb2.loc.gov/cgi-bin/query/I?brhc:18:./temp/~pp_XUCi::displayType=1:m856sd=cwpbh:m856sf=00710: @@@mdb=fsaall,app,brum,detr,swann,look,gottscho,pan,horyd,genthe,var,cai,cd,hh,yan,bbcards,lomax,ils,prok,brhc,nclc,matpc,iucpub,tgmi - Salmon P. Chase

"2 cent coin." No date. Online image. http://en.wikipedia.org/wiki/United_States_Two_Cent_Coin PD - 2-cent coin

"$500 note." No date. Online image. www.moneyfactory.gov/section.cfm/5/61US Treasury Bureau of Engraving and Printing - $500 note

"$1000 note." No date. Online image. www.moneyfactory.gov/section.cfm/5/61 US Treasury Bureau of Engraving and Printing - $1000

"$5000 note." No date. Online image. www.moneyfactory.gov/section.cfm/5/61 US Treasury Bureau of Engraving and Printing - $5000

"$10000 note." No date. Online image. www.moneyfactory.gov/section.cfm/5/61US Treasury Bureau of Engraving and Printing - $10000

"Rev. Duche." No date. Online image.http://lcweb2.loc.gov/cgi-bin/query/I?fsaall,app,brum,detr,swann,look,gottscho,pan,horyd,genthe,var,cai,cd,hh,yan,bbcards,lomax,ils,prok,brhc,nclc,matpc,iucpub,tgmi:2:./temp/~pp_NwN4::displayType=1:m856sd=cph:m856sf=3a05055:@@@mdb=fsaall,app,brum,detr,swann,look,gottscho,pan,horyd,genthe,var,cai,cd,hh,yan,bbcards,lomax,ils,prok,brhc nclc,matpc,iucpub,tgmi- Painting

"Seal." No date. Online image. http://www.photolib.noaa.gov/historic/c&gs/images/big/theb1449.jpg noaa. PD-USgov- seal

"In God We Trust." No date. Online Image. Secret Service. Retrieved September 5, 2004.http://www.secretservice.gov/money_design_features.shtml - Dollar bill logo

"Continental Currency."http://en.wikipedia.org/wiki/Image:Continental_Currency_One-Third-Dollar_17-Feb-76_obv.jpg PD

"Coho Salmon."http://www.photolib.noaa.gov/fish/images/big/fish3010.jpg PD. Originally from "The Fishes of Alaska." Bulletin of the Bureau of Fisheries, Vol. XXVI, 1906, P. 360, Pl XXXII.

"William McKinley." No date. Online image. www.moneyfactory.gov/section.cfm/5/61 US Treasury Bureau of Engraving and Printing - William McKinley

"Grover Cleveland." No date. Online image. www.moneyfactory.gov/section.cfm/5/61 US Treasury Bureau of Engraving and Printing - Grover Cleveland

"James Madison." No date. Online image. www.moneyfactory.gov/section.cfm/5/61 US Treasury Bureau of Engraving and Printing - James Madison

"Salmon Chase." No date. Online image. www.moneyfactory.gov/section.cfm/5/61 US Treasury Bureau of Engraving and Printing - Salmon Chase

"Sunrise." Photo by M.D. Mitchell. Used by permission.

Letter H:

"Soldiers." Used by permission. Library Company of Philadelphia.

"High Street." No date. Online Image. http://lcweb2.loc.gov/cgi-bin/query/D?ils:3:./temp/~pp_wk9B:@@@mdb=fsaall,app,brum,detr,swann,look,gottscho,pan,horyd,genthe,var,cai,cd,hh,yan,bbcards,lomax,ils,prok,brhc,nclc,matpc,iucpub,tgmi

"Carpenter's Hall." No date. Online image. Beyond DC. Retrieved September 7, 2004. http://www.beyonddc.com/galleries/Philly/images/100_1376.jpg - Carpenter's Hall

Letter I:

"Signing of the Constitution". No date. Online image. http://teachpol.tcnj.edu/amer_pol_hist/thumbnail78.html PD

"'Rising Sun' Chair." Independence National Historical Park

"'Rising Sun' Chair." Independence National Historical Park

"General John Burgoyne." No date. Online image. http://en.wikipedia.org/wiki/Image:John_Burgoyne.jpg PD

"American Gothic a la Peter."

"The Battle of Bennington." Chappel, Alonzo. Bennington Museum, Bennington, Vermont - Battle of Bennington picture

"Annie and Winston," Judy Mitchell

Letter J:

"William Taft's tub." No date. Online image. http://www.wellswooster.com/phototaft.htm Used by permission - William Taft's tub

"William Howard Taft." No date. Online image. http://www.americaslibrary.gov/jb/reform/jb_reform_taft_1_e.html - William Howard Taft

"Supreme Court Building." JFM. Photos used with permission.

"Old City Hall of Philadelphia." No date. Online image. http://teachpol.tcnj.edu/amer_pol_hist/fi/00000061.htm :PD

"John Jay." Gilbert Stuart, 1795. Online image. http://teachpol.tcnj.edu/amer%5Fpol%5Fhist/fi/00000057.htm; PD

"Cass Gilbert." No date. Online Image. Library of Congress, http://lcweb2.loc.gov/cgi-bin/query/D?ils:1:./temp/~pp_dl7e::@@@mdb=fsaall,app,brum,detr,swann,look,gottscho,pan,horyd,genthe,var,cai,cd,hh,yan,bbcards,lomax,ils,prok,brhc,nclc,matpc,iucpub,tgmi - Cass Gilbert

"John Marshall." William James Hubbard, c. 1832. Online image. http://en.wikipedia.org/wiki/Image:CJMarshall.jpg PD-art

"Ethan." From the collection of Mark Mitchell. 2003.

Letter K:

"King George III." No date. Online Image. http://en.wikipedia.org/wiki/Image:George_III_of_the_United_Kingdom-e.jpg PD

"Charlotte Mecklenburg Strelitz". No date. Online image.http://en.wikipedia.org/wiki/Image:Charlotte.jpg#file PD - Charlotte Mecklenburg Strelitz

"Nathan Hale." Used by permission. The Connecticut Historical Society Museum, Hartford, CT - Nathan Hale

"Buckingham Palace." Paul Hofman. Used by permission.

"Charles I" 1600-1649. Online Image. http://en.wikipedia.org/wiki/Image:Carolus_I.jpg PD- Charles I

"George Washington." Stuart, Gilbert. 1795. Online Image. http://lcweb2loc.gov/cgi-bin/query/D?ils:36:./temp/~p_Lg7b::@@@mdb=fsaall,app,brum,detr,swann,lookgenthe,var, cai,cd,hh,yan,bbcards,lomax,ils,prok,brhc,nclc,matpc,iucpub,tgmi PD

Letter L:

Lillback, Peter A. Proclaim Liberty...a Broken Bell Rings Freedom to the World. Bryn Mawr, PA: The Providence Forum, 2001. – Liberty Bell

"Villanova University Chapel". M.E. McMorrow. Used with permission - Villanova University Chapel

"Copperhead Snake." Alan Journet. Used with permission. No date. Online image. http://cstl-csm.semo.edu/journet/persprof/LIDNfauna.htm - copperhead snake

"Samuel Adams." No date. Online Image. http://en.wikipedia.org/wiki/Image:SamuelAdamsLarge.jpeg PD- Samuel Adams

"Old Augustine Church Philadelphia." Colin Ryder. Used by permission. http://www.colinryder.com/travel/us/pa/philadelphia/page12.html - Old Augustine Church Philadelphia

"Inscription."Lillback, Peter A. Proclaim Liberty...a Broken Bell Rings Freedom to the World. Bryn Mawr, PA: The Providence Forum, 2001. – Liberty Bell Inscription

Letter M:

"Timber Rattler." Special thanks to Dr. Ned Gilmore, Academy of Natural Sciences, Philadelphia, PA- Timber Rattler

"Benjamin Franklin". No date. Online Image. http://encyclopedia.laborlawtalk.com/Image:Benjaminfranklin.jpg - Benjamin Franklin

"Join or Die." Library of Congress, http://lcweb2.loc.gov/cgi-bin/query/D?ils:1:/temp/~pp_U8eD::@@@mdb=fsaall,app,brum,detr,swann,look,gottscho,pan,horyd,genthe,var,cai,cd, hh,yan, bbcards,lomax,ils,prok,brhc,nclc,matpc,iucpub,tgmi -Political cartoon

"Navy Jack Flag". No date. Online image. http://commons.wikimedia.org/wiki/Image:Naval_Jack_of_the_United_States.svg PD - Navy Jack Flag

"Massachusetts Spy". No date. Online image. Library of Congress, http://lcweb2.loc.gov/cgi- pp_gviE::@@@mdb=fsaall,app,brum,detr,swann,look,gottscho,pan,horyd,genthe,var,cai,cd,hh,yan, bbcards,lomax,ils,prok,brhc,nclc,matpc,iucpub,tgmi - Massachusetts Spy

"Christopher Gadsden". No date. Online Image. Historycentral.com. Retrieved November 30, 2004. http://www.historycentral.com/Bio/RevoltBIOS/GadsdenChristopher.html - Christopher Gadsden

"Army Seal." No date. Online Image. Institute of the Heraldry - Army Seal

"Rattlesnake seal". No date. Online image. Retrieved November 30, 2004. http://www.gadsden.info/clipart.html - Rattlesnake seal

Letter N:

"John Adams." No date. Online Image. http://en.wikipedia.org/wiki/Image:JohnAdams.jpg PD - John Adams

"Mountain beaver." Audubon , John J. 1845-48. Online Image. Lewis-clark.org. Retrieved September 26, 2005. http://www.lewis-clark.org/media/NewImages/BOBCAT/an_mtn-beaver-audubon.jpg

"John Bartram's garden." Online Image. Courtesy of Bartramsgarden.org. Retrieved April 12, 2005.www.bartramsgarden.org/see/index.html/house_bushes.jpg - John Bartram's family garden

"Alexander Wilson." No date. Online Image. Sully, Thomas. http://en.wikipedia.org/wiki/Image:Wilson_Alexander_1766-1813.jpg PD - Alexander Wilson

"William Bartram." Online Image.http://en.wikipedia.org/wiki/Image:WilliamBartram.jpeg PD - William Bartram

"Franklinia alatamaha." No date. Online Image. Used by permission. Bartramsgarden.org. Retrieved April 12, 2005.www.bartramsgarden.org/images/franklinia/frank.engraving.jpg - Franklinia alatamaha

"Benjamin Franklin." No date. Online image. http://commons.wikimedia.org/wiki/Image:Benjamin_Franklin_by_Jean-Baptiste_Greuze.jpg PD - Benjamin Franklin

"Meriwether Lewis." No date. Online Image. http://en.wikipedia.org/wiki/Image:MeriwetherLewis.jpeg PD - Meriwether Lewis

"Telescope." Online Image. Missouri Historical Society, St. Louis –William and Clark Collection. Photograph by David Schultz. Used by permission. Telescope

"William Clark." No date. Online Image. http://en.wikipedia.org/wiki/Image:WilliamClark.jpeg PD - William Clark

"Thomas Jefferson." No date. Online Image. http://www.answers.com/topic/thomasjefferson-jpg PD - Thomas Jefferson

Photo & Picture Credits

Letter O:

"Santa Claus," http://en.wikipedia.org/wiki/Image:1881_0101_tnast_santa_200.jpg PD - Santa Claus

"A Live Jackass Kicking a Dead Lion," Nast, Thomas. January 15, 1870. Online image. Harper's Weekly. Retrieved February 3, 2005. http://cartoons.osu.edu/nast/kicking_lion.htm

"Nast signature." No date. Online image. Used by permission: The Thomas Nast Society. Retrieved February 3, 2005. http://www.jfpl.org/nast.htm - Nast signature

"Elephant." The Granger Collection. Used by permission

"Common Sense." No date. Online Image. http://en.wikipedia.org/wiki/Image:Commonsense.jpg PD - Common Sense

"Thomas Paine.": Online image. Auguste Millière (1880), after an engraving by William Sharp, after a portrait by George Romney (1792) http://teachpol.tcnj.edu/amer_pol_hist/fi/0000002c.htm PD

"Soap box." No date. Online Image. Used by permission: Sydow's Antiques. Retrieved February 3, 2005. http://www.sydowsantiques.com/hcat12.htm - Soapbox

"Paine's gravestone." No date. Online image. Cape Cod Gravestones. Retrieved February 3, 2005. http://www.capecodgravestones.com - Paine's gravestone

"Andrew Jackson." No date. Online image. http://www.whitehouse.gov/history/presidents/images/aj7.gif, PD - Andrew Jackson

"Abraham Lincoln." No date. Online image. http://en.wikipedia.org/wiki/Image:Abraham_Lincoln_head_on_shoulders_photo_portrait.jpg- PD- Abraham Lincoln

"Daniel Webster." No date. Online image. teachpol.tcnj.edu/amer_pol_hist/fi/0000008e.htm, PD - Daniel Webster

Letter P

"John Witherspoon."No date. Online image. http://en.wikipedia.org/wiki/Image:John_Witherspoon3.jpg, PD

"Tusculum." No date. Online Image. photo credit: Gary Nigh www.rootsweb.com. Retrieved February 8, 2005. http://www.rootsweb.com/~njmercer/Site/Tusculum.htm - Tusculum

"Richard Stockton." No date. Online Image. United States Attorney Office, District of New Jersey. Retrieved February 8, 2005. http://www.usdoj.gov/usao/nj/history.html - Richard Stockton

"Dr. Benjamin Rush." No date. Online Image. http://en.wikipedia.org/wiki/Image:Benjamin_Rush_Painting_by_Peale.jpg PD- Dr. Benjamin Rush

"Dr. Joseph Warren." No date. Online image. http://en.wikipedia.org/wiki/Image:Joseph_warren.gif , originally from: https://www.cia.gov/csi/books/warindep/photo-12.gif PD

"Benedict Arnold." No date. Online image. The National Archives. Retrieved February 8, 2005. http://www.archives.gov/research/american-revolution/pictures/images/revolutionary-war-139.jpg - Benedict Arnold

"William Henry Harrison on a horse."Anne S. K. Brown Military Collection, Brown University Library. Used by permission.

Letter Q

"Queen Elizabeth." Online Image."The Ermine Portrait" of Elizabeth I of England. 1585 by Nicholas Hilliard. http://es.wikipedia.org/wiki/Imagen:Elizabeth1England.jpg PD -Queen Elizabeth 1

"Elizabeth with Scepter. " No date. Online image.- http://en.wikipedia.org/wiki/Image:Elizabeth_I_of_England_-_coronation_portrait.jpg PD- Elizabeth 1

"Elizabeth's signature." No date. Online image. http://en.wikipedia.org/wiki/Image:Autograph of Elizabeth I of England %28from Nordisk familjebok%29.png-signature PD - signature

"Heath's Memoirs." No date. Online image. Used by permission: Michael Brown Rare Books, LLC. Retrieved February 9, 2005. http://www.mbamericana.com/Heath2.jpg - Heath's Memoirs

"Sir Francis Drake." After 1590. Online image. http://commons.wikimedia.org/wiki/Image:1590_or_later_Marcus_Gheeraerts%2C_Sir_Francis_Drake_Buckland_Abbey%2C_Devon.jpg PD- Sir Francis Drake

"Walter Raleigh and son." No date. Online image. http://upload.wikimedia.org/wikipedia/commons/6/6a/WalterRaleighandson.jpg PD - Raleigh and Son

"Sir Walter Raleigh." Online image. 1585. Nicolas Hilliard. http://es.wikipedia.org/wiki/Imagen:Nicholas_Hilliard_005.jpg PD - Sir Walter Raleigh

"Queen Henrietta Maria." Online image. 1636/38. Anthonis van Dyckhttp://es.wikipedia.org/wiki/Imagen:HenriettaMariaofFrance02.jpg PD - Queen Henrietta Maria

"Farthing." No date. Online image. Used with permission. Chris Perkins http://www.predecimal.com/images/farthing.jpg- Farthing

"The Colonies Reduced." 1767. Online image. http://lcweb2.loc.gov/cgi-bin/query/I?fsaall,app,brum,detr,swann,look,gottscho,pan,horyd,genthe,var,cai,cd,hh,yan,bbcards,lomax,ils,prok,brhc,nclc,atpc,iucpub,tgmi:1::/temp/~pp_zam1::displayType=1:m856sf=3a35351:@@r mdb=fsaall,app,brum,detr,swann,look,gottscho,pan,horyd,genthe,var,cai,cd,hh,yan,bbcards,lomax,ils,prok,brhc,nclc,matpc,iucpub,tgmi- The Colonies Reduced

"Crown" Online image. http://etc.usf.edu/clipart/2100/2114/crown_1.htmFile Name: crown_1 from John J. Anderson A School History of England (New York: Effingham Maynard & Co., 1889) PD

"Queen Christina." No date. Online image. http://people.bu.edu/wwildman/WeirdWildWeb/courses/wphil/lectures/wphil_theme13.htm PD- Queen Christina

Letter R

"Capitol building." No date. Online image. http://es.wikipedia.org/wiki/Imagen:USCapitol.jpg PD

"U.S. Capitol." Online Image. Thomas U.Walter, "Elevation of the Dome of the U.S. Capitol." 1859. Library of Congress. http://www.loc.gov/exhibits/us.capitol/kkseven.jpg public domain

"Noah Webster." No date. Online image. http://en.wikipedia.org/wiki/Image:Noah_webster_small.png PD- Noah Webster

"The Blue-backed Speller." No date. Online image. Used by permission. www.visionforum.com - The Blue-backed Speller

"The Head and Helmet of the Statue of Freedom". No date. Online image. Crawford, Thomas. The Architect of the Capitol. Retrieved on February 23, 2005. Used by permission.

"Benjamin Franklin." No date. Online image. http://pt.wikipedia.org/wiki/Imagem:Franklin-Benjamin-LOC.jpg PD - Benjamin Franklin

"Yale University." No date. Online image. http://en.wikipedia.org/wiki/Image:Original_Yale_College_Building.jpg PD - Yale University building

Letter S

"Telescope." No date. Online image.Asa Smith. before 1923. http://upload.wikimedia.org/wikipedia/en/8/86/Refractor_Cincinnati_observatory.jpg PD - Telescope

"Dice." 2003. Online image. photo credit: Steven Eggerling, SJESoft.com. Retrieved March 1, 2005. http://www.sjesoft.com/3DGallery/trueSpace/dice.jpg - dice

"Francis Hopkinson." No date. Online image. http://en.wikipedia.org/wiki/Image:Francis_Hopkinson_sepia_print.jpg PD - Francis Hopkinson

"USS Constellation." No date. Online image. Texas Philatelic Association. Retrieved March 1, 2005. http://www.texasphilatelic.org/resources/stamps2004/constellation.jpg - USS Constellation stamp

"Great Seal Impression." 1782. Online Image. Great Seal die. http://en.wikipedia.org/wiki/Image:GreatSealofUS%2CFirstDie.gif PD from National Archives - Great Seal Impression

"Great Seal."-Thomson, Charles. 1782. Online image. http://encyclopedia.thefreedictionary.com/_/viewer.aspx?path=9/99/&name=Great_Seal_of_US,_Verso_Design,_1782.png - Great Seal

"USS Constellation in Baltimore." Joe Webster (www.joewebster.net) http://en.wikipedia.org/wiki/Image:20040725_USS_Constellation_Baltimore.jpg PD- USS Constellation in Baltimore

Letter T

"Liberty Tree ." © Marion Warren. No date. Online image. The Annapolis Publishing Company. Retrieved March 7, 2005. http://www.annapolisbooks.com/posters/index.cfm - Used with permission

"Liberty Tree." No date. Online image. Sons of Liberty Chapter, Sons of the American Revolution. Retrieved March 7, 2005. www.sons-of-liberty-sar.org/newsletters.html - Boston Liberty Tree

"Broadside posted by the Sons of Liberty." 1770. Online image. http://memory.loc.gov/cgi-bin/query/r?ammem/rbpebib:@field(NUMBER+@band(rbpe+03700300)) Library of Congress, Rare Book and Special Collections Division

"Paul Revere Statue." No date. Online image. http://en.wikipedia.org/wiki/Image:Paul_Revere_Statue_by_Cyrus_E._Dallin%2C_North_End%2C_Boston%2C_MA.JPG PD- Paul Revere Statue

"Liberty Pole." Johann Wolfgang von Goethe, 1793. http://en.wikipedia.org/wiki/Image:Freiheitsbaum.jpg, PD - liberty pole

"Paul Revere." Copley, John Singleton.1768. Online image. http://en.wikipedia.org/wiki/Image:J_S_Copley_-_Paul_Revere.jpg PD- Paul Revere

"Alexander Hamilton." No date. Online image. http://en.wikipedia.org/wiki/Image:Alexander_Hamilton.jpg PD - Alexander Hamilton

"King's Chapel." No date. Online image. Edsen Breyer's Postcard Museum. Retrieved March 7, 2005. http://www.ebpm.com/bost/bigpix/fan_bostking002.html - King's Chapel, Boston

"Coast Guard Ensign." Wolcott, Oliver. 1799. Online image. Director of Auxiliary 7th Coast Guard District. Retrieved March 7, 2005. http://www.dirauxwest.org/uscg-flags-ensign.htm - Coast Guard Ensign

Letter U

"Virgil." No date. Online image. http://www.hberlioz.com/Photos/BerliozPhotos8a.html - Virgil

"E Pluribus Unum." Thomson, Charles.1776. Online image. www.loc.gov/exhibits/us.capitol/eleven.jpg- E Pluribus Unum

"Map of the 13 American Colonies." 1775. rs6.loc.gov/gmd/gmd371/ g3715/g3715/ct000001.gif PD from Library of Congress Geography and Map Division.

"United Colonies Currency." 1775. Online Image. "courtesy of the Federal Reserve Bank of San Francisco" - United Colonies Currency

"Spanish 8 Reales." 1753. Online image. www.celebrateboston.com/images/gallery/pillar.jpg - Spanish 8 Reales

"Metacomet." No date. Online image. http://en.wikipedia.org/wiki/Image:King_Philip%2C_by_Revere.jpg PD - King Philip

"Swansea, Massachusetts seal." No date. Online image. photo credit: Sandra M Clark, Retrieved March 16, 2005. http://www.swanseamass.org/history.html - Swansea, Massachusetts seal

"Crispus Attucks." No date. Online image. Used by permission. The Crispus Attucks Association of York Pennsylvania.The Learning Company 1997 - Crispus Attucks

Photo & Picture Credits

...Activity Pages

THE GREAT SEAL FRONT

golden glory
breaking through a cloud
yellow with
white clouds

13 silver stars on
blue ground, one
for each of the 13
colonies

Out of many, one
banner
cream-colored

bald eagle
(national symbol)
brown body &
wings, white
head

E PLURIBUS

UNUM

olive branch with
13 leaves and 13 olives
(symbol of the power
of peace that Congress holds)
green leaves, brown olives

bundle of 13 arrows
(symbol of the power
of war that Congress holds)
brown arrows

shield without any other supporters
denotes that the United States of America
ought to rely on their own virtue
blue top, red & white stripes

Eye of Providence
triangle (symbol of
trinity) in blue, aura in gold

"He (God) has favored
our undertakings"
letters in gold on a blue field

unfinished pyramid
symbol of strength
and duration
colored in
light tan

ANNUIT

COEPTIS

MDCCLXXVI

NOVUS ORDO SECLORUM

tan background

"A new order of the ages"
words on a gold banner

1776
the date of the
Declaration of Independence,
the beginning of the new
American Era

COLOR THE AMERICAN FLAG

red stripe   red stripe   red stripe   red stripe   red stripe   red stripe   red stripe

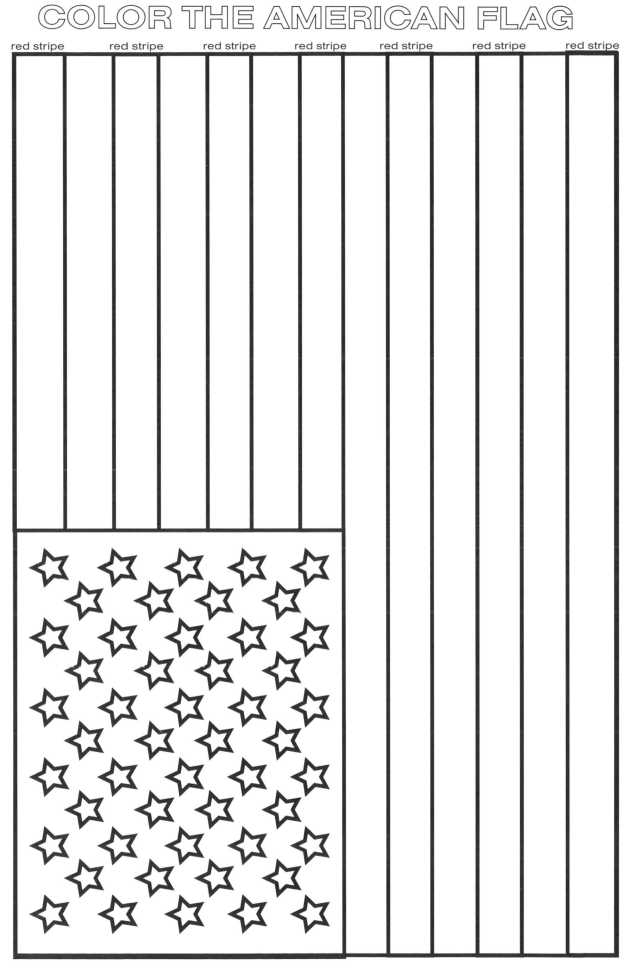

field of blue

HOW TO FOLD THE FLAG

Step-by-step instructions to properly fold Old Glory

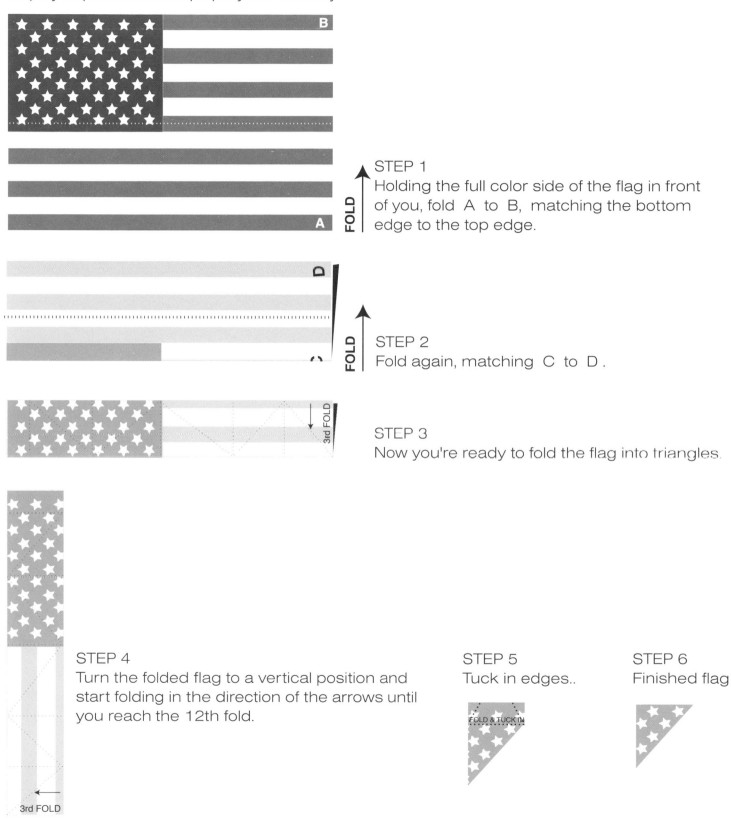

STEP 1

Holding the full color side of the flag in front of you, fold A to B, matching the bottom edge to the top edge.

STEP 2

Fold again, matching C to D.

STEP 3

Now you're ready to fold the flag into triangles.

STEP 4

Turn the folded flag to a vertical position and start folding in the direction of the arrows until you reach the 12th fold.

STEP 5

Tuck in edges..

STEP 6

Finished flag

The Providence Forum has created a "foldable" flag with which you can learn how to fold the flag properly and the meaning of each fold. To receive your own copy, please contact us at 1.866.55FORUM or visit us at www.providenceforum.org.

THE MEANING OF THE FLAG'S FOLDS

The following is the meaning for each of the flag's folds:

The first fold of our flag is a symbol of life.

The second fold is a symbol of our belief in the eternal life.

The third fold is made in honor and remembrance of the veterans departing our ranks who gave a portion of life for the defense of our country to attain peace throughout the world.

The fourth fold represents our weaker nature; for as American citizens trusting in God, it is to Him we turn in times of peace as well as in times of war for His divine guidance.

The fifth fold is a tribute to our country, for in the words of Stephen Decatur, "Our country, in dealing with other countries, may she always be right, but it is still our country, right or wrong."

The sixth fold is for where our hearts lie. It is with our heart that we "pledge allegiance to the flag of the United States of America, and to the republic for which it stands, one nation under God, indivisible, with liberty and justice for all."

The seventh fold is a tribute to our Armed Forces, for it is through the Armed Forces that we protect our country and our flag against all enemies, whether they be found within or without the boundaries of our republic.

The eighth fold is a tribute to the one who entered into the valley of the shadow of death that we might see the light of day, and to honor our mother, for whom it flies on Mother's Day.

The ninth fold is a tribute to women, for it has been through their faith, love, loyalty, and devotion that the character of the men and women who have made this country great has been molded.

The tenth fold is a tribute to father, for he, too, has given his sons and daughters for the defense of our country since they were first born.

The eleventh fold, in the eyes of Hebrew citizens, represents the lower portion of the seal of King David and King Solomon and glorifies, in their eyes, the God of Abraham, Isaac, and Jacob.

The twelfth fold, in the eyes of Christian citizens, represents an emblem of eternity and glorifies God the Father, the Son, and Holy Ghost.

When the flag is completely folded, the stars are uppermost, reminding us of our national motto, "In God We Trust."

After the flag is completely folded and tucked in, it takes on the appearance of a cocked hat, ever reminding us of the soldiers who served under General George Washington and the sailors and marines who served under Captain John Paul Jones who were followed by their comrades and shipmates in the Armed Forces of the United States, preserving for us the rights, privileges, and freedoms we enjoy today.

THE DOLLAR BILL

DID YOU KNOW?

Our "paper" currency is made from 25% linen and 75% cotton with red and blue fibers scattered throughout. It measures 2.61 inches wide by 6.41 inches long and has an average lifespan of 18-22 months. Old, worn bills are shredded. The back is printed in green; hence, the dollar bill has been nicknamed the "greenback."

The portraits of those on our paper currency were chosen in 1928. Though there is no record of why they were selected, it is only fitting that George Washington, our first president, "first in war, first in peace, first in the hearts of his countrymen," would be placed on the one dollar bills.

There are two sets of seals engraved on each side.

The obverse side has a seal with the name of a city that is home to a Federal Reserve Bank surrounding a letter (A - Boston, B - NYC, C - Philadelphia, D - Cleveland, E - Richmond, F - Atlanta, G - Chicago, H - St. Louis, I - Minneapolis, J - Kansas City, K - Dallas, L - San Francisco).

On the other side is the Treasury Seal with scales, symbolizing a balanced budget. Nice thought.

"In God we trust" is on all of America's currency. These words were placed on the nation's coins in March 1865, the final act of President Abraham Lincoln before his assassination one month later.

The reverse side shows the two sides of The Great Seal.

CAN YOU FIND.....  steps on the pyramid, stars above the eagle, bars on the shield, leaves on the olive branch, arrows?

WHAT ARE THE THREE LATIN PHRASES? DO YOU REMEMBER WHAT THEY MEAN?
(See below for answers.)

_____   _____   _____

OOOOO....WHAT IS _THIS_? _____

WHAT DOES THIS NUMBER MEAN? MDCCLXXVI **WHY IS IT SIGNIFICANT?**

1776, the date of our independence from England
The all-seeing eye of Providence

Annuit Coeptis (He has smiled on our undertakings), E Pluribus Unum (out of many, one), Novus Ordo Seclorum (a new order of the ages)

ANSWERS:

75

CUT YOUR OWN 5-POINTED STAR

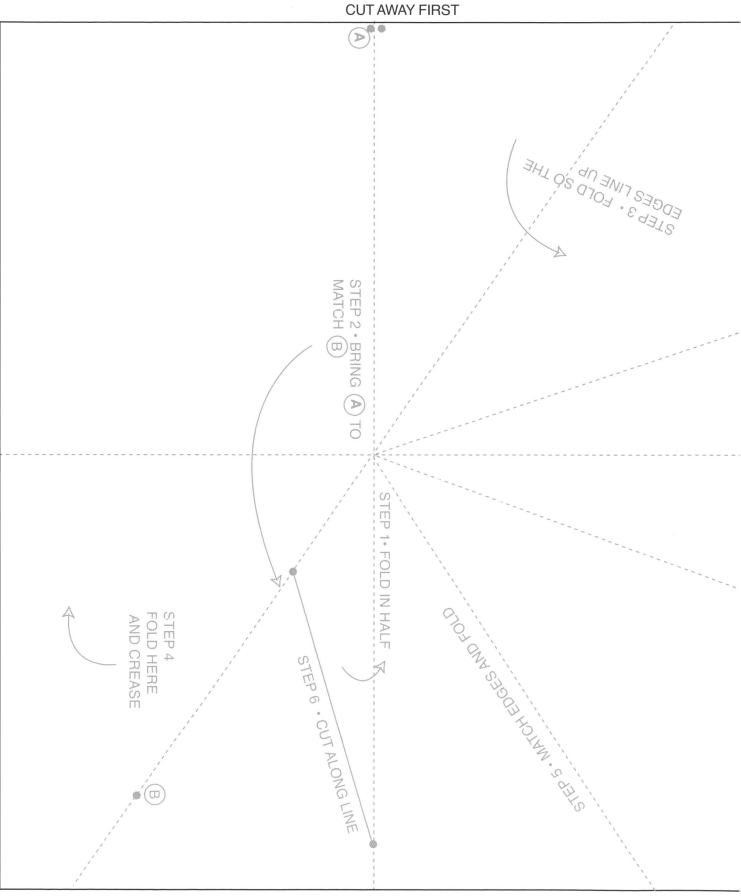

STEP 3 · FOLD SO THE
EDGES LINE UP

STEP 2 · BRING Ⓐ TO
MATCH Ⓑ

STEP 1 · FOLD IN HALF

STEP 4
FOLD HERE
AND CREASE

STEP 6 · CUT ALONG LINE

STEP 5 · MATCH EDGES AND FOLD

It is recommended that you make copies of this page. Lighter weight paper is easier to fold and cut
AND just in case the first star is less than perfect, you'll have more with the instructions printed on them.

GENERAL HEATH'S LOST FLAGS

The next 3 flags were based on sketches found in the papers General William Heath written by during his time of service in the Continental Army (see Letter Q). His drawings depicted ideas which were to be used to create flags representing the ideals that guided the early patriots.

This flag tell us that the defense of the Colonies (the 13 arrows) is a virtue. Its reward from Heaven is liberty, represented by the liberty cap coming down from above (see Letter L).

An oft-used symbol for American freedom, this victorious native warrior smiles as he stands over a fallen white horse. The tyranny they resisted was that of King George III, whose ancestral coat of arms, from the House of Hanover, included a white horse.

This pure white flag with the single word "purity" on it was the last of the flags General Heath proposed. In his view, the struggle for liberty against tyranny was born of pure motives. The color white was the traditional color for purity and innocence. Choose a color for the word "purity."

Draw your own flag of liberty. Think carefully about the symbols and colors you choose. Why do they best represent your ideas of freedom?

LESSONS on LIBERTY
A Primer For Young Patriots

NOTES